INSTANT DECORATING

INSTANT
Decorating

Original ideas for transforming a room in hours

Stewart Walton and Elizabeth Wilhide

Special Projects by Claire Lloyd

Special Photography by Richard Foster

CONRAN OCTOPUS

First published in 1993 by
Conran Octopus Limited
37 Shelton Street, London WC2H 9HN

British Library Cataloguing-in-
Publication Data
A catalogue record for this book is
available from the British Library.

ISBN 1 85029 398 8

Typeset by Servis Filmsetting
Limited, Manchester
Printed in Hong Kong

Project Editor *Simon Willis*
Editorial Assistant *Michael Williams*
Copy Editor *Jane Royston*

Art Editor *Helen Lewis*
Illustrations *Lynne Robinson,
Stewart Walton*
Picture Researcher *Jessica Walton*

Production Controller *Jill Macey*

**PUBLISHER'S
ACKNOWLEDGMENTS**
The publisher would like to thank
the following for their assistance
with this book: Michelle Clark; Dylon;
Matthew Usmar Lauder; and Mathers
and Powell, London.

Special thanks to **Arthur Sanderson
and Sons Ltd, London** for supplying
the paint used in the special projects.

INTRODUCTION

INTRODUCTION

Everyone knows how creating a beautiful home is supposed to be: painstaking preparation with layer upon layer of undercoat; silky smooth finishes sanded and honed to perfection; expertly lined and weighted drapery with intricate hand-sewing; professionally tailored upholstery with all the trimmings; and delightful displays of well-chosen, recherché *objects. The exquisite and tasteful result will reflect a lifetime's diligent application.*

Decorating can seem terribly intimidating. Judging by the wealth of publications pouring forth advice and glossy images, it can also be hideously expensive and exceptionally time-consuming. At the very least, you will need a degree in art history and a diploma in advanced DIY to bring your own four walls up to an acceptable standard of taste and finish. An unlimited amount of funds, all the free time in the world and a charming period property will also come in handy.

The truth, thankfully, is very different. The secret of successful decorating, as many people are increasingly aware, is neither time, nor money, nor specialized skills – but imagination. Some of the most exciting and original effects are the results of flashes of inspiration hastily executed on a wet Sunday afternoon, or brilliant exercises in lateral thinking that cross-fertilize ideas, techniques and materials from different disciplines in a sudden burst of innovation and creativity.

This book is for those people with little money and even less time, but who have a creative urge to bring sparkle to the dull corners of their homes. It is for new home-owners with little spare change in their pockets; students who want to give their rented flat a face-lift; those whose time for DIY is only as long as a baby's nap; or those whose enthusiasm flags at the second undercoat. It is for those who vow to do it 'properly' one day ... but not yet.

Cheap and Cheerful

If you can't afford to replaster walls to create an immaculately smooth surface for decorating, exploit the textural effect of a rough finish. This uneven pink-painted wall has a forthright style – beautiful in its own right (left)**. Paint supplies the suggestion of architectural detail in the form of a simple free-hand dado** (right)**.**

The nannying tone of much decorating advice makes departing from the straight and narrow seem risky. But what such worthy professionalism conceals is that taking shortcuts is itself a professional approach. Photographic stylists and set designers conjure bravura effects with simple techniques and materials. And there are plenty of interior decorators whose best efforts owe more to an impetuous moment than a lifetime's expertise.

There is room for both approaches. But there is a time in most people's lives when resources are stretched and instant decorating is the only alternative to none at all. And for those wedded to textbook methods, the instant approach is a reminder that decorating can – and should – be fun.

GETTING STARTED

SOURCES OF IDEAS

The instant decorator can take heart that many decorative effects and even some historical styles owe a great deal to a spirit of improvisation. In the past, when materials were rare, expensive or hard to come by, people had to make do with what was to hand and the robust, exuberant results of this approach often seem more vital and appealing today than the virtuoso displays of fine craftsmanship in more stately surroundings.

Early American colonists, for example, working to establish their settlements in hard conditions, had little leisure and no money to import expensive luxuries such as hand-printed wallpapers from Europe. Instead, using coloured limewash, earth colours and even soot, they stencilled their own simple hand-cut patterns directly on to walls or panelling, over fireplaces and on furniture, a vivacious and free interpretation of the rhythm and structure of traditional wallpaper designs. And in some cases, paint was daubed on freehand in remarkable splodges and graphic blots – revealing with an endearing directness a deep desire for decoration whatever the limits of present circumstances.

Away from court circles and grand country houses, such ingenious economies were usual. Vernacular traditions of decoration sometimes copied in cheaper materials what might be finely executed in luxury ones, but equally often displayed their own forthright style of decoration, handed down through generations. Rough walls washed in brilliant colour or chalky white, homespun textiles set off with the simplest trimming, quilts and rugs pieced with scraps and snips of fabric, stylized natural or geometric patterns, and the soothing harmonies of stone and wood and clay are the basic elements we have fashioned into country style today: an instant vocabulary of simple, cheap decoration.

Around the world, many of these vernacular traditions persist, a source of ideas for every instant decorator. Paint, easy to use and cheap, is the basis for much decorative gaiety. Along the shores of the Mediterranean and Caribbean, brilliant partnerships of white, sea-greens and blues, hot pinks and rich ochres underscore architectural detail, singing out on painted shutters and doors. Zigzag patterning inside an African mud hut, the scorching clash of pink and magenta on a Mexican verandah, dashing pillarbox red windowframes and whitewashed walls on an Irish cottage are examples that vividly illustrate simple means of enrichment.

Art is another potent inspiration, whether it takes the form of calligraphic squiggles and dots painted free-hand on the wall for a Matisse-like background; Cocteau-inspired flights of fancy with mirror, fake leopardskin and voluminous drapery; or solid blocks of primary colour for Mondrian modernism.

All kinds of 'found' objects, beautiful and free, can be the basis for a decorative theme. Sea shells piled in a glass jar or ranged on a window-sill are a popular form of display; or you could go further and use the shells as decoration, sticking them on to a mantelpiece or threading them on to muslin curtains. Similarly, packing trunks could be revamped as seating or low tables; battered baskets, waterings-cans and pails all make excellent containers.

One piece of advice often given in decorating books is to keep a scrapbook of ideas: pages torn from magazines, postcards, scraps of fabric or ribbon – anything which attracts you for its colour, pattern or ingenuity. This may feel wincingly self-conscious at first, but it will help you decide what you really like and will build up a fund of ideas to spark your imagination. More importantly, it can save a great deal of time when you are trying to think what to do with the spare room and your mind suddenly goes blank.

Favourite Things

An essential element of instant decorating is the display of favourite things. A collection of figures and animals is set off by a vivid turquoise background (opposite above).

Authentic Decor

There is a good historic precedent for painting wooden furniture (opposite below).

Seashore

A beachcomber's treasure trove is a fine example of 'themed' improvisation.

PREPARATION

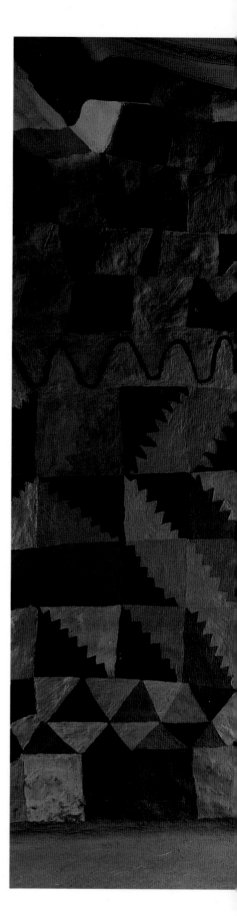

Before you begin, it is wise to be aware of what instant decorating can't do. It goes without saying that no amount of decorating is going to correct the effects of serious structural faults (the kind that result in large cracks, sagging floors and seeping damp stains), although some superficial concealment may be possible. Really poor surfaces – pitted, holed and cracked – will only be hidden by sticking something else – such as paper, fabric or wood – over the top. The dull truth is that sound, time-consuming preparation is necessary for smooth, even finishes, sharp corners and true edges.

Instant decorating is not a strategy for perfection or a panacea for all decorating ills, but it is a way of using shortcuts and sideways jumps to make the most of limited resources. It is unlikely that your starting point will be a perfectly prepared surface: and if not, the end product won't be either. But it will be lively, cheerful and infinitely more pleasing to live with than it was before.

How little basic preparation you can get away with is a critical issue, and is something that manufacturers are constantly addressing with their ranges of one-coat paints, non-drip solid emulsions and quick-drying varnishes. Modern paint covers a multitude of sins: on walls you can assume that hairline cracks and small irregularities will be less noticeable and that general griminess will disappear after a coat or two. For gloss-painted or varnished woodwork, a little sanding is all that is required to provide a key for a new coat of paint. And if a country look is what you're after, painted furniture often looks more authentically rustic if the cracks aren't all filled or the imperfections sanded away.

Provided that the cracks are not crevices, the irregularities are not craters and the skirting-boards are not clogged with layers of tacky gloss, basic repainting will freshen and improve any surface immeasurably for just a small amount of time and trouble. One

African Zigzag

The urge to decorate one's surroundings is universal, transcending limitations of material and circumstance. Bravura patterning transforms the walls of an African mud house. Bold chevrons, zigzags and toothed edging carried out in the warm palette of natural earth colours – terracotta, rust, rich brown and buff – express a tribal exuberance.

proviso is that you do not try to save money by choosing cheap paint: this is always a false economy. It does not cover well, so more coats are needed; it streaks and smears, so colour is uneven. And don't ever be tempted to prise open a tin of paint and slap it straight on without first brushing down the surface to remove loose dirt, dust and cobwebs or without covering yourself and adjacent surfaces to protect against spills and splashes.

The same holds true for other aspects of instant decorating. Spend a few minutes assembling whatever tools and materials you will need to complete the job, move furniture out of the way if necessary and cover up what you can't move. A few minutes spent being sensible and organized at the outset will save you hours trying to get paint out of the carpet or glue off the upholstery later on.

BENDING THE RULES

Instant decoration really comes into its own in the use of materials and tools. DIY shops are stacked with dozens of brushes for every conceivable application, together with impossibly technical-looking tools and equipment with little indication as to their ultimate purpose. For the confused amateur, such displays are as likely to sap confidence as to empty the wallet.

The list of basic tools you will need to complete most decorating jobs is actually quite short. Good paintbrushes are essential: wide for tackling large surface areas and narrow for trims and details. Rollers speed up large painting jobs, and foam rollers can be cut to create instant special effects. Ordinary artists' brushes – synthetic will do just as well as sable – are ideal for adding fine decorative detail. Pencils, a ruler and tracing-paper are needed for setting out stencil patterns and other preparatory work, while masking tape saves time in cutting around trim and details.

Many accessories can be improvised from what you already have around the home. A bucket or old roasting tin serves as a receptacle for paint; old saucepans or large jars are useful for mixing colours. An old plate makes a good palette for mixing shades for decorative details. Spare rolls of plain lining-paper or wooden offcuts are invaluable for trying out ideas.

Paint effects are essentially improvised – the result of decorators trying out different materials and tools in order to achieve a particular result. Old rags, kitchen cloths, chamois leathers, bathroom sponges, toothbrushes, nailbrushes, household brushes and brooms are just some of the ad-hoc tools that have been used to create the dappled, stippled and streaked colour effects that have become so fashionable in recent years. You can buy an expensive stippling brush from a specialist decorators' suppliers, but if a cut-down household brush does the job, why spend the money?

You may, however, like to invest in a number of tools not normally associated with traditional decorating. A staple gun, for example, is necessary for some of the 'soft-furnishing' projects described in this book. Glue guns are another standby of set design and window display which also have a place in instant decoration. Spray-painting is, naturally, quicker than brush-painting, and can transform techniques such as stencilling. Other tools and materials mentioned during the course of this book are unlikely to be more obscure than coloured felt-tipped pens or upholstery nails.

As far as paint is concerned, emulsion (water-based) paint is better for basic decoration than oil-based paints such as eggshell or gloss, even for painting furniture. Emulsion is quick-drying and with a pleasing finish that recalls the chalkiness of old-fashioned, home-made paints; its spills and splashes are also much easier and less time-consuming to clear up afterwards.

All White

A monochromatic palette simplifies decorating decisions and effortlessly creates a mood of serene sophistication. Chairs wrapped in white sheeting acquire a mysterious presence of their own – an economical, washable and easily renewed form of covering when new upholstery would break the budget.

COVERING UP

Tackling large surface areas – walls, ceilings and floors – is usually a daunting prospect. But even if resources are limited, it is worth getting the background right, as any improvement here will have a beneficial effect on the whole room.

Backgrounds don't have to be boring. The purpose of many paint effects and techniques is to create a quiet, shimmering surface with a pattern, texture or subtle modulation of colour that gives depth and atmosphere. It is usually a good idea to keep walls, ceilings and floors fairly low key, and then to splash intense spots of colour on furnishings, pictures or objects.

Braver souls may still find it hard to resist a bold approach. Walls drenched in strong colour can have an unbeatable vitality that lifts any room out of the ordinary, but it takes a sure touch to keep all the elements under control.

Whichever strategy you adopt, take a cold hard look at the basic features of the room before you begin. What is worth enhancing, and which aspects need to be disguised? You may want to supply architectural distinction in the form of a paper frieze or a painted or stencilled pattern at cornice height. Awkward angles and irregularities can be dissolved with a flowing, all-over pattern, while if surfaces are simply too poor to paint, consider covering them completely using paper or fabric.

Attention to detail is often taken as a way of urging perfection, and perfection is often what the instant decorator cannot afford. Even small items can cost a surprising amount. If you have to be economical you can devote your efforts to the details that really make a difference, and save worrying about the rest until later.

Fast Work

Simple all-over patterns quickly cover large areas. Try stencilling gold stars over a midnight-blue background (above). **Graphic blots daubed on a white wall show how early American settlers utilized basic materials** (right), **while free-hand dots and a painted frieze provide a mellow background** (far right).

COLOUR

Colourways

The decoration here makes a virtue out of necessity, picking out angles and planes in different colours. This bold strategy helps to compensate for the lack of fine architectural detail (far right).

Instant Dado

The dado is traditionally covered in a different material from the wall above. In default of panelling or textured paper, this dado makes use of lines and squiggles, cross-hatched in paint (above).

Once you have worked out a basic strategy for redecorating your room, the next decision is likely to concern colour. As far as interiors are concerned, most of us have had our ideas on colour shaped by the marketing departments of paint manufacturers. We are accustomed to thinking in terms of colour cards, those sheets of innumerable tinted squares that seem to offer every possibility but are in reality so intimidating and inhibiting.

In practice, by far the best way to understand the power and potential of colour is to forget about colour cards altogether and to experiment with colour-mixing yourself. In this you can be guided by the advice that art teachers generally give their students: namely, to start with a limited palette and build up a thorough appreciation of all the subtle half-shades and mixtures that can be achieved using only a small selection of colours.

The most basic form of colour-mixing is simply to add a tint to white. A spoonful of colour mixed into a pot of white emulsion will give you the same type of tinted white that is enthusiastically promoted by paint companies. The colour that you add to the emulsion base can consist of anything, provided that it is water-soluble: more emulsion, coloured ink, artists' stainers, gouache (opaque watercolour), food or fabric dye – even cold coffee or turmeric. It is worth experimenting with 'found' colour to create unusual shades. The one basic rule that you must follow is that water-based products can be mixed and oil-based products (such as gloss paint, eggshell, undercoat and artists' oils) can be mixed, but oil and water never mix. As well as creating colours, you can also achieve really

interesting textures. Mixing opaque paint and transparent varnish in the ratio of about one part paint to ten parts varnish, for example, results in a milky finish similar to limewash once it has dried and been rubbed back using wire wool or a scrubbing-brush.

This type of one-step colour-mixing is ideal for creating a single colour or texture. Going a stage further, mixing two complementary colours and white will give you a family of related shades, enough to develop the basis of an interesting decorative scheme.

Colour theory can take you into the abstruse realms of optics and applied psychology. For decorative purposes, it is enough to understand that each colour has an opposite or complementary colour. Red is paired with green, blue with orange, and yellow with purple. When these pairs are used together in their pure, intense forms the result is electric and vibrant. This 'chemistry' of colour relationships is exploited in all of the most successful contemporary decorating schemes.

You can see how the process works by choosing two complementaries and trying out different combinations. If you choose a red and a green, for example, they may not be perfectly matched in tone or intensity. But if you mix a small quantity of the green into the red and a small quantity of the red into the green, the two new colours will automatically be linked. To take the mixture a shade lighter, add white; to darken it, add more of the complementary colour. If you continue the process of mixing the colours in different ratios, you will eventually build up a whole family of related colours, from pastels to sludgy tones, all of which will work well together.

Surface Design

Classical Stripe

Tented rooms decorated in striped fabric were the height of fashion in the early nineteenth century. A hint of this military style is achieved using broad chalky blue stripes painted on the wall and by the simply draped metal bedstead (above).

Paint effects are ideal for instant decoration. Many of these improvised techniques evolved as ways of imitating something too expensive to use, notably marble, granite and other luxurious materials. Spattering, sponging, stippling, scumbling, ragging and graining may sound like esoteric branches of the decorator's art, but they are nothing more than ways of making textured paint marks or patterns on a surface.

In the realm of paint finishes, it is easy to become obsessed with different methods and recipes, tools and paint mixtures. But what really counts is achieving the finish you want, not how you get there. You can work free-hand if that proves more effective, or use a combination of methods or tools. If you

forget about recipes and concentrate on the process of pattern-making, you may surprise yourself with an interesting result you hadn't anticipated.

Experiment with different household brushes, rags, sponges and scraps of fabric, dipping each in paint and testing the print in a sheet of lining-paper to see which effect you like best. Cut up foam rollers to make instant stripes, or cut sponges into shapes for printing. Scrubbing-brushes can be cut into as well to make a ragged, non-mechanical striping akin to graining.

What most of these methods have in common is that they produce a broken-colour finish in which the base coat shows through a patterned top layer. For the amateur, it is best to keep the top coat close in tone and colour to the

Borders

Photocopied leaf-prints trim a stripey paint effect made from a cut roller (above).

Subtle tones

Paint effects are often best in subtle near-shades, such as pale yellow on white. For the amateur, mistakes will be less obvious and the final effect more sophisticated than bold contrasts. Broad stripes can be painted easily and quickly using paint rollers – vary the size according to the width you require (above).

base coat. This is because success with these techniques relies on the ability to cover the ground consistently and evenly; and so if the two colours are closely related, then mistakes and smudges will be less obvious.

Colour-washing with a weak solution of water-based paint is a quick way of adding some instant colour or modifying an unattractive wall shade. You can tone down an egg yellow, for example, with sweeping strokes of diluted red on a large brush, without losing the essential warmth of the original shade. The obvious brushmarks that result from this method are part of the charm of the finish. In general, it obviously saves time if you can work with an existing background in this way, rather than repainting it completely. This is

especially true if the wall is dark in tone, as several light-coloured coats would be needed to cover it up.

Colour-washing is also one of the techniques that can be used to age a surface artificially. It may seem positively perverse to go to the trouble of simulating the effects of wear and decay, but what professionals like to call the 'patina of age' can be very appealing. Ageing a surface by washing it with several related earth-tones, or creating crazed or crackled effects with flecks of undercolour, can result in finishes with great depth and character. Making a virtue of imperfections is easier than starting from scratch, and these mellow yet lively backgrounds are less demanding of perfection than other areas of decoration.

Textured Paint

These broad textured panels, crisply defined by areas of plain paint, make an interesting variation on a stripey theme. The distressed effect can be achieved by removing flecks and patches of wet paint with a dry roller (above).

Painted Plaid

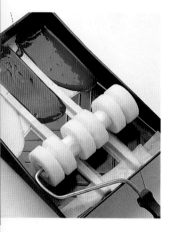

Tartan Roller

Cut a paint roller into three equal sections, binding masking tape in between to keep them separate. Then tie each section in half with string. Divide a paint tray into sections corresponding to the cuts in the roller; use strips of plastic or batten secured with waterproof tape (above). Fill each section with a different colour. Add water if the paint is too thick. Roller the verticals first, lining up by eye with the corner of the wall. Wait about ten minutes, then roller the horizontals.

Oil and Water

Paint falls into two main categories: water-based (emulsion) and oil-based (gloss, eggshell and undercoat). Water-based paints are thinned with water and can be coloured by adding any other water-soluble paint or substance (watercolour paints, acrylic, gouache). Oil-based paints are thinned with white spirit and can be coloured using artist's oils. It is vital to remember that oil and water don't mix.

PAINT EFFECTS

Colour-washes

A tinted wash can be applied over any water-based painted background. The basic recipe is water and acrylic varnish in the ratio of about 2:1. Mix up a little water-based colour – watercolour, inks, gouache – to a thin, creamy consistency and test the colour before adding to the wash. A wash with less water has more body.

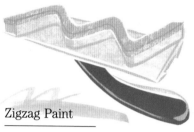

Zigzag Paint

This zigzag effect is created with a proprietary paint pad cut to shape with a sharp knife and daubed randomly over a flat painted background. Test out prints first on scraps of paper to achieve the effect you want (left).

Diamond Paint

A rugged all-over diamond print is the result of using a paint pad cut as shown above, applied in vertical bands across a background. Ready textured rollers, of the type used to apply 'artex' finishes, can also be worth trying out (right).

Brushwork

Paintbrushes can be cut and shaped to make bold patterns in paint (left)**. An ordinary decorator's brush is cut into three sections to make a randomly applied finish. These effects often work particularly well when background and foreground colours are similar in tone.**

Glazes

Oil-based glazes take longer to dry than washes, and spills are more difficult to clear up. But the glowing, luminous effect can repay the extra effort. Mix white spirit with oil-based varnish in the ratio of about 2:1, and add oil-based colour to suit. Reducing the amount of solvent (white spirit) will create a glaze that has more body.

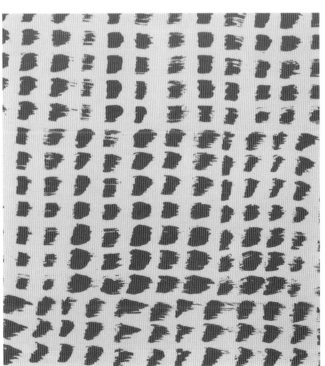

Checkerboard

A paperhanger's brush, normally used to apply wallpaper paste, is wide enough to allow a series of 'teeth' to be cut. Experiment with paint consistency and pattern spacing to find the right effect (left)**.**

PAPERING OVER

Some surfaces are beyond cosmetic improvement and require more radical measures. Covering up the offending wall or walls is one option that falls within the scope of the instant decorator. Lining walls with fabric requires patience and a degree of skill; although such transformations are highly effective, they are by no means instant, while wallpaper for a large room can be expensive. The answer is to look for inspiration in cheap sources of paper and other collage materials.

With ordinary wallpaper paste and a willingness to experiment, you can paper a wall with almost anything. Pages from comics, sheets of newspaper (the pink *Financial Times* is particularly effective), maps, menus, playbills, sheets of music, Japanese or Chinese calligraphy all produce lively and graphic all-over patterning. This type of treatment should be used with discretion, but works particularly well in a small room such as a study or downstairs lavatory.

For a more sober effect, brown wrapping-paper can make a surprisingly elegant background. Cheap textured papers (such as the kind often used by florists to wrap flowers) are equally good, or you could collage torn layers of fine coloured tissue, sealed with a coat of varnish for protection. A photocopier is also a useful tool if you want to recreate the look of the traditional print room, with its cut-out enrichments and engravings stuck directly on to a subtly coloured background.

Scrim

Scrim, the open woven mesh used by plasterers to seal the joints between plasterboard, is an unlikely choice for decorating, but the bold texture of this cheap and commonplace material acquires an intriguing look when pasted on a wall (right).

Newspaper

The vertical emphasis of columns of newsprint shows how the daily news can stand in splendidly for wallpaper. Use wallpaper paste sparingly, so as not to soak the paper, and take care to align columns of text as accurately as possible. An instant finishing touch is provided by a zigzag frieze of corrugated paper stencilled with a basic flower shape (right).

Mapping it Out

Map-reading

All kinds of maps, sea charts and star guides make interesting substitutes for wallpaper. The two approaches shown here illustrate the range of possibilities. The patched assembly of individual old faded maps and charts makes a muted background for a study area (left), **while a children's room has been papered in an educational and eye-catching large-scale world map** (right). **When using any printed material to cover the walls, bear in mind that words written in your own language inevitably draw the eye and invite you to read what they say, while foreign language sources are less immediately recognizable and are consequently less insistent.**

SIGNED AND SEALED

Cut and Paste

Antique title deeds and other handwritten documents which turn up in junk-shops can provide the raw material for papering a wall. Here, photocopies of the same bond have been used to cover the wall of a study. Apply wallpaper paste to each sheet, stick in position and brush out any air bubbles with a sponge or paintbrush. When the prints have dried in place, apply a thin coat of water-based tinted varnish to give an antique appearance. Apply the varnish unevenly with a medium-sized paintbrush; if the result is not dark enough, wait an hour and apply a second coat.

Sourcebook

The images shown on these two pages, all of which are out of copyright, make good starting points for photocopied effects. Use the copier to enlarge, reduce and multiply; you can experiment with friezes, borders or repeat patterning.

QUESTIONS OF SCALE

Headed Paper

Classically inspired, this black-and-white wallpaper features alternately large- and small-scale heads of Roman emperors (left). **The effect recalls traditional print rooms with their cut-out engravings pasted on to the wall. A similar look could be achieved by photocopying and cutting out a favourite image in two different sizes to repeat around the room.**

Figure Frieze

Imitate the boldness of this expensive wallpaper by montaging photocopies of historical characters on to a wall. Reproduction ceiling roses stuck to the wall provide a bold architectural frieze (left). **Use the photocopier to make enlargements for all-over papering, good for lampshades as well as the wall** (above).

ARCHITECTURAL DETAIL

If unsympathetic conversion has stripped away all the architectural detail in a room – the cornices, brackets, architraves, ceiling roses and so on – it is relatively straightforward to reintroduce at least some of them. Reproductions of classic mouldings and embellishments are widely available, either in plaster (which can be expensive), or else in cheap, lightweight polystyrene. Although polystyrene versions sound cheap and nasty, they are very easy to install and, once up on the wall and painted, look surprisingly convincing. The plainer styles with simple profiles are generally best.

Wooden moulding is versatile. A strip of beading will neatly cover any gap that may have opened up between skirting-board and floor. Moulding can be applied high up the wall as a picture-rail, or just under halfway down as a dado rail, although it is meaningless to add the latter if you don't then go on to treat the lower portion of the wall in a different way with paint, paper or panelling. As long as you are using the moulding simply to provide a decorative form of punctuation, you can simply glue it in place using an aliphatic resin adhesive although nailing it will give a more permanent result.

Deep, mitred beading can give a flush door the look of a panelled door, making an instant standby if you can't afford to replace modern doors with solid originals. If the door has some architectural merit, pick it out in colour or try out a decorative effect such as graining, which is traditionally associated with woodwork. Wood stain is a good way of retaining the pattern of grain while adding colour.

FIRST IMPRESSIONS

In the wider scheme of things, halls and entrances count as detail. It's easy enough to exhaust your creativity and your cash on the living-room or kitchen and neglect to improve the area just past the front door at all. But while you won't spend much time there, the hall has a disproportionately large effect on the way both you and your visitors are likely to feel about your home, easing the transition from outdoors to in.

To begin with, a hall should give some kind of flavour or hint of what is to come, either through its colour or decorative effect. Strong, positive colour is often avoided in hallways and on stairs because it can limit colour choices in the rooms opening on to these connecting areas.

Very little in the way of furniture will fit into the average hall; in any case, clutter is best kept to a minimum. A narrow table is a good place for the post – better than piling it all in a heap on the stairs – as well as for a jug of flowers, making a refreshing sight for everyone coming and going during the day. Even if your hall furniture is limited to a telephone table and a chair, some sort of punctuation point is better than a featureless corridor.

Star Panels

The effect of panelling can be created at a fraction of the cost by applying ready-made wooden mouldings to the wall and treating the enclosed areas in a simple decorative way, as here with its bright stencilled stars (left).

Architrave

Lateral thinking is called for when you need to compensate for a lack of good architectural detail. You can add interest to what would otherwise be featureless doorways by painting the inner surfaces of plain doorways in a distinctive colour (right).

Stairway

The simple device of outlining a stair with a strip of contrasting colour makes up for the absence of defining mouldings or trim (above). **The same strategy can be used to paint in a skirting or to frame a doorway.**

PICKING OUT

Sea View

A deeply recessed window is given extra definition by a border of starfish, stuck straight on to the rough plastered wall. The marine display in the window reveal reinforces the theme (right).

A quick way to transform a room is to add coloured or patterned detail around the margins. Friezes, borders and painted banding all inject a graphic quality to the decoration, lending definition and crispness. If the basic surfaces are in pretty good condition but lack zest, this type of detail can make a great difference.

Positioning is all-important. Natural breaks occur between the ceiling and wall, where a cornice would be; at picture-rail height; about a third up from the floor, where a dado rail would be; and at skirting-board level.

Since only a relatively small surface area is involved, this type of detail can be bright and bold without running the risk of swamping the rest of the decoration. If the walls are quiet, a line of complementary colour or black will sharpen up the effect. A frieze of stencilled motifs or sprayed-on stars can supply the type of interest normally supplied by plasterwork flourishes, while a dado patterned in paint will set up a lively opposition to an expanse of plain wall above. Painted-on skirtings are a common feature of many vernacular interiors. A rich terracotta colour taken about 20cm (8 inches) up the wall extends the tiled floors of rustic Italian villas visually and helps to disguise knocks and scrapes to the base of the wall.

More fanciful ideas include festooning swags of objects united by a common theme and sprayed white to look like plaster; raiding suppliers of decorative detail for cherubs or other forms of sculptural relief; or sticking on stars and bosses to make bold punctuation points. Photocopiers come in useful for blowing up details to make pasted-down borders and friezes (see page 34). And you can print single motifs with almost anything – cut-up potatoes and sponges are excellent for making naive shapes of animals to march around nursery walls.

The antithesis of crisp architectural detail – such as free-hand wiggly lines, dots and chevrons – can be incredibly effective when used to trim and accentuate the top of a wall. On warm ochre, terracotta or colour-washed walls, this type of uninhibited decoration has a distinctly tribal appeal.

Fresco

A toothed painted frieze and mottled paint effect are excellent ways of compensating for, respectively, the lack of a cornice and poorly finished walls (right).

FLOORS

If your floorboards really need covering up but you can't afford carpeting or tiles, you can paint them instead. Floors coated with matt oil-based paints make ideal surfaces for stencilling a range of designs on. Widely spaced laurel wreaths give subtle decorative covering (far left)**. Stylized flower shapes strike a handsome, rustic note** (left)**, while random fish prints look lively under foot** (right)**.

One new home-owner, impecunious after buying her flat, found that she could not stand the sight of the old carpet in the living-room, with its luridly swirling, stomach-churning pattern. In a brilliant flash of inspiration, she turned the carpet over and discovered that the hessian backing made a hard-wearing and perfectly acceptable base material for rugs, as unobtrusively elegant as sisal matting.

Not all flooring problems are so neatly solved, but there are a surprising number of cheap and cheerful ideas to improve matters underfoot. Simplicity is generally the best policy where floors are concerned, especially since most treatments are labour-intensive and time-consuming. Plain scrubbed floorboards with a scattering of cotton dhurries or rag rugs look infinitely better than cheap carpeting which will thin and age unattractively within the year. A more unusual version of this basic combination is to lay strips of rag runner along the main pathways through your rooms in a manner reminiscent of Scandinavian farmhouses.

Large sheets of plywood screwed in place make an appealing modern floor. Plywood can be very easily stained, stencilled and varnished to increase decorative possibilities. In the same way, hardboard laid with the smooth side up and sealed with a couple of coats of clear or tinted varnish has the seamless sophistication of expensive linoleum floors.

When fine carpeting was even more costly than it is today and synthetic materials had not been invented, painted floorcloths were the economical alternative. The process of making a floorcloth is a little too laborious for the average amateur, but paint is still a good means of covering up poor floorboards or adding decorative flourishes in the form of stencilled borders and stylized motifs. You will need to use tough, oil-based paint on the floor if it is to wear well (yacht paints provide the best results). Although such finishes will take several days to dry, during which time the room will be out of use, the labour and expense involved are much less than those required to sand and seal old boards.

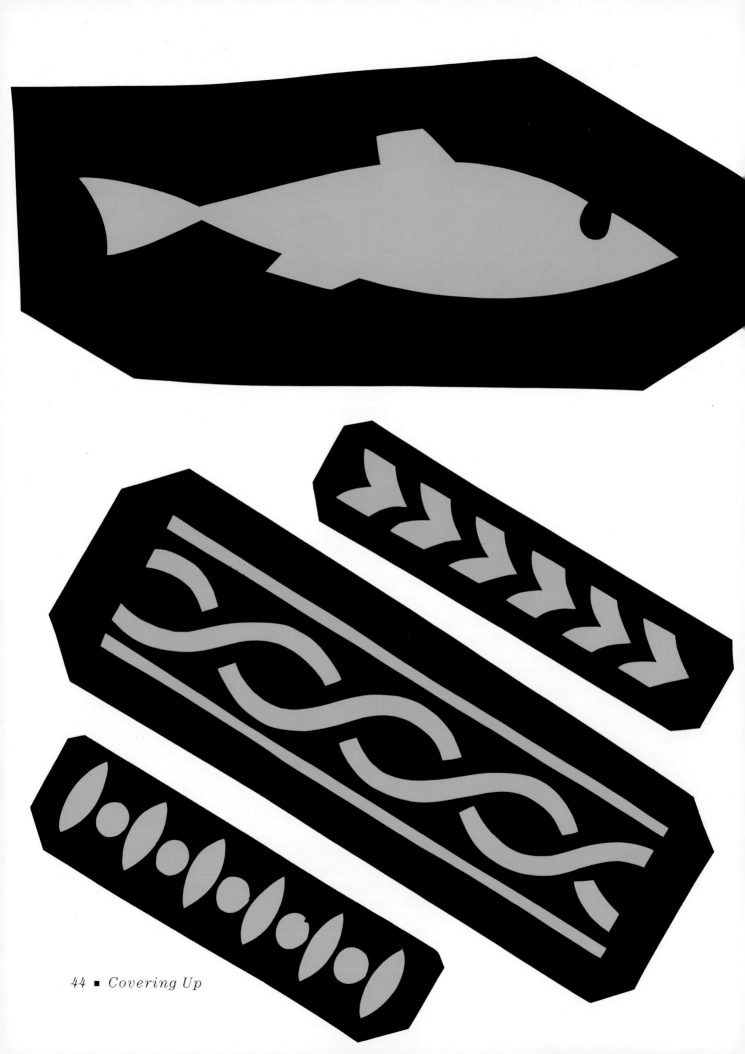

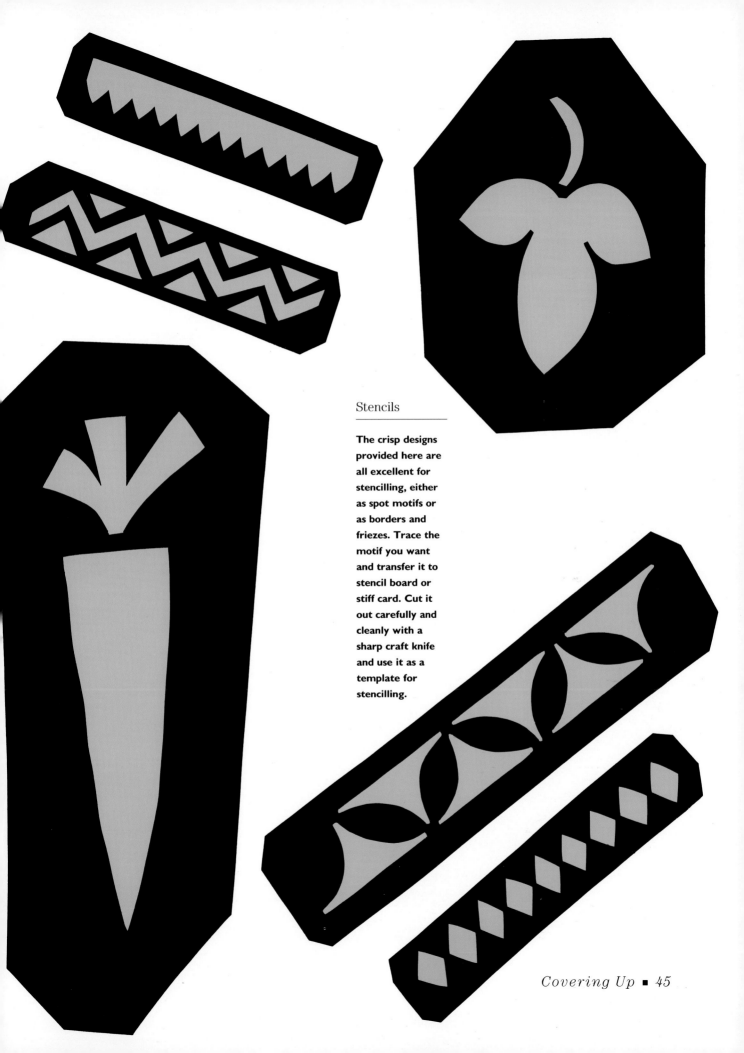

Stencils

The crisp designs provided here are all excellent for stencilling, either as spot motifs or as borders and friezes. Trace the motif you want and transfer it to stencil board or stiff card. Cut it out carefully and cleanly with a sharp craft knife and use it as a template for stencilling.

WINDOW DRESSING

Window Dressing

Many people are deterred from tackling window treatments by the received wisdom that the undertaking will devour their decorating budget. But despite their potential expense, they do offer great scope for originality and creative economy. And you don't have to be accomplished with a needle and thread to come up with dazzling effects that look every bit as impressive as the very height of soft-furnishing fashion.

Despite the relatively small surface areas involved, windows cannot be ignored. The focal point of any room, windows draw the eye, either by virtue of their architectural character or the view that they reveal. What is more, window treatments provide a natural opportunity to display colour, pattern and texture and to reflect the decorative style of the room, which is why so much effort and expense tend to be devoted to them.

In a very few cases, the whole issue can be side-stepped by doing without any covering at all. If the window is finely detailed, filled with beautiful stained glass or if it is an unusually graceful shape (and if privacy and screening light are not important) the window can simply be displayed in all its glory. Most windows, however, demand some kind of dressing, if only for practical reasons. And few people are entirely comfortable at night in a room in which there are no curtains or blinds to draw against the dark.

Nothing suggests luxury more than soft folds of fabric falling to the ground in a graceful sweep, or billowing festoons floating over the top of the window frame. But don't despair if your budget does not stretch to elegant chintz with all the trimmings. The

impression of luxury depends more on being generous with the amount of fabric than on the price per metre. The secret of creating sumptuous window treatments in an economical and effective way is to exploit the versatility of fabrics and materials not usually associated with soft furnishings.

FABRICS

If you are looking mainly for decorative impact, basic cottons such as muslin, calico and cotton voile are a good starting point. Plain cotton is cheap, so you can indulge in metres of it. It is also light and easy to work with which makes it ideal for many quick-sewing or non-sewing techniques. And it can be printed, dyed, stencilled and trimmed to your heart's content.

There is nothing new about using light, filmy drapery at windows. Many contemporary paintings of eighteenth-century interiors show muslin, lace or light cotton either in conjunction with festoons or richer material or, as was often the case in summer months, as a substitute for them. In northern countries, where summer light was so welcome after the interminable gloom of winter, many windows featured the merest slip of lace or muslin crowning the top of the frame, a little flourish in fabric rather than a full-scale covering. There is something inherently charming about the contrast between the ordered classicism of such rooms and their furnishings, and the light, fresh simplicity of the window-dressing.

Light cottons are not the only option. The smooth, dense sateen-type of material normally used for lining can make stylish curtains in its own right, particularly as it is now available in a range of colours aside from the basic

Plain Sailing

This window fills almost the whole wall with little room at the sides or at the top from which to attach any covering. The neat solution uses lengths of cheap plain cotton simply tacked in place and drawn up in soft wings of fabric. Extra light control, essential in a bedroom, is provided by roller blinds (left).

WINDOW DRESSING

neutral buffs and greys. Lining silk is also surprisingly affordable, although it may need to be weighted with a fringe or other trimming to make it hang properly. Striped, cotton mattress ticking is hard-wearing, economical, fresh and contemporary. Indian bedspreads patterned with 'Tree of Life' or paisley designs would work well as curtains in a room with a Victorian or ethnic style of pattern. Felt is yet another possibility: it comes in a range of brilliant shades for warmth and depth of colour. Sailcloth or unprinted artist's canvas both share a sculptural quality when hung in stiff folds, and are ideal for nautical-style blinds.

Antique curtains are no longer the bargain buy they once were, as those in good condition command relatively high prices. But junk-shops and second-hand stalls are still a good source of odd bolts of fabrics left over from the 1930s, '40s and '50s, which would make an authentic and cheerful contribution to a retro-style room.

Don't neglect dress fabrics. Lengths of plaids, ginghams, stripes and spots can sometimes be picked up on the remnant table and put to decorative use at the window. Fabrics blended with a percentage of man-made fibre often make good lightweight drapery, and the pattern ranges available are generally good. For a really theatrical effect, saris are unbeatable. Simply drape them over the window, where the light shining through will intensify their iridescent colour, their pattern and glittering detail.

Light Touch

Filmy muslin has a long history of use as a window treatment, traditionally as lightweight undercurtains to filter bright sunshine. But this pretty semi-transparent fabric looks good enough on its own and is so economical you can afford to be generous with the amount (far left).

Drapery

A bolt of glorious crimson glazed fabric, draped in deep swags over a pole and caught up to the left in an asymmetrical arrangement, adds to the Baroque splendour of this period room. When draping a window, it may take several attempts before you are satisfied with the way the fabric hangs (left).

CURTAINS

At the simplest level, most materials can be draped over a pole or metal curtain rod to create something of the look of swags and tails. Lightweight cottons and semi-transparent fabrics can be knotted and swathed in all kinds of ways; heavier material may need a few retaining stitches or staples to keep the folds in place. The special virtue of these effects is that they are easy to dismantle, either for cleaning or if you just want to try something new.

If you would rather have curtains that can be drawn, there are several ways of making headings that involve minimal sewing. One basic method is to make a cased heading which gathers the fabric up into soft folds as it is drawn along a pole or rod. To do this, simply fold down a hem at the top of each curtain and sew along the edge to create a channel of fabric, then thread the curtain on to the pole.

A variation on the same theme, which suits fabric with more body, is to cut into the casing to make scalloped or crenellated shapes. Alternatively, you can attach loops of tape at intervals along the top of the curtain, sew on brass rings, or eyelet the top of the curtain and thread ribbon or tape through to lace the fabric to the pole. To create a curtain with its own integral pelmet, attach rings or tape to the back of the curtain some distance down from the leading edge and allow the top to flop over in soft folds. Make sure the heading is strong enough to support the weight of material. Incidentally, all these ideas can be adapted for doorways or beds. When calculating the amount of fabric, allow for hems at the top and bottom; curtains that draw need a fabric width of one and a half to two times the window width.

French Windows

Dress fabrics may not be as durable as conventional furnishing materials but they provide a good source of colour and pattern, often at a fraction of the cost. To make these sumptuous curtains for french windows, a bottle-green synthetic taffeta was chosen for its silky finish and iridescent colour. The 'curtains' are unheaded and attached to the curtain pole by means of sprung metal clips, which allow them to be gathered in folds. The 'pelmet' consists of another length of fabric draped over the pole; tasselled ropes make tie-backs, and a small amount of material bunched in the hand into a 'rose' and stapled in place provides the finishing touch.

53

Decorating and Trimming

Cotton is easy to dye; in fact, it was this quality that originally made it so popular as a furnishing fabric. Dip bright white muslin or new lace in tea for a soft, naturally aged tone, or dye plain cotton any shade under the sun to fit in with an existing decorative scheme. Muslin and other cottons also print well; the homespun look of the weave can be accentuated by naive block prints of animals, fish, shells and other natural shapes. In a more sophisticated vein, classical designs such as stylized acanthus leaves stencilled in off-white on to snow-white muslin recreate the subtle textured look of fine damask. There are also excellent fabric paints available which enable you to paint free-hand directly on to cloth.

You can further customize basic fabric with a whole range of trimmings – traditional and otherwise. Light muslin – widely used at the windows in early nineteenth-century Biedermeier rooms – was often graphically set off with black knotted or bobble-cotton fringing. Haberdashers as well as furnishing departments are a good source of ideas for livening up simple drapery.

Braid, bias binding, ribbon and woven cotton tape can be sewn or glued on in rows across the hem of a curtain or blind, or right around the fabric to edge it in colour. Bright yellow shapes appliquéd on to midnight-blue felt make a Matisse-style backdrop. If, as in this case, you use a light-coloured fabric appliquéd on to a darker base fabric, cut away the base fabric from beneath the newly applied piece to maintain the bright contrast in colour. For a shimmering, light-catching effect, you could sew or stick on sequins, small mirrors or glass beads. Even sea shells can look great sewn on to muslin or toile (linen-cloth). Many shells already have small pinholes which make it easy to thread them.

Vibrant Colour

A shocking pink scarf and its equally shocking yellow partner provide a jolt of colour contrast to liven up a plain window. Plain muslin scarves are cheap and easy to dye bright colours, and you can trim the lower edge, as here, with glass beads for extra decorative quality and style (right).

Sari Splendour

For instant glamour and glitter, saris are hard to beat. Many of the more luxurious examples are encrusted with metallic embroidery which catches the light for a sparkling effect. If the material is very light, you may need to weight the lower edge so that the drapery hangs flat (right).

GLITTERING GOLD

Starstruck

Make no-sew curtains with a dramatic star print using lengths of standard black interlining (the material used to make curtains light-proof). Measure the distance between the curtain rod and the floor and allow enough fabric for each curtain to rest in soft folds on the ground. Cut star shapes from folded paper (opposite) **in the pattern you desire and use the shape to cut a stencil template out of stiff card. Then spray the stars on to the matt side of the fabric using car spray paint. Gather up each curtain and attach at intervals using pinch clips available from upholstery outlets.**

PELMETS AND ACCESSORIES

Check Pelmet

Pelmets, fixed in place and covering a portion of the window, do not have to be elaborately constructed or tailored to be effective. Fabric can be fixed along the top edge to a batten and trimmed or cut along the lower edge for a dash of extra style (right).

Spotty Pelmet

This deep pelmet in spotty fabric is edged by a wide border in a bold animal-skin print. Iron-on interfacing or fabric stiffener attached to the back of the fabric allows it to be cut out to make a fancy decorative edge (right).

Most of the simplest drapery and curtain styles in this book will leave the curtain pole or rod in full view (conventional headed curtains are generally designed to be used with track which is hidden by a pelmet). If your fabric and curtain style are inherently plain and unfussy, you can play up the element of contrast by going over the top with your accessories.

Wooden poles can be painted, stained, gilded or varnished; they can be improvised using dowelling and customized by sticking on wooden or metal finials. For an ultimately rustic look, suspend a branch of weathered driftwood from the windowframe to support a length of billowy muslin or a simple blind (see page 64–5). You could also dress up a basic metal rod with finials at either end, decorative brackets, cleats and other paraphernalia for a look of instant Regency grandeur. Gilt and brass accessories can be very expensive – particularly antique ones – but you can salvage all kinds of interesting bits and pieces of ironmongery to achieve a similarly impressive effect.

Solid pelmets that project over the top of the curtain to hide the heading and track are often nothing more elaborate than fabric-covered boxes. Stiff card or polyboard is easy to cut and shape, and can do the job just as well as wood panels: with fabric stretched over a layer of padding, stapled into place around a simple wooden frame and trimmed with braid, few people will notice the difference. Or you can experiment with building up layers of corrugated cardboard for a bold sculptural effect (see page 61).

Ropes and tasselled cords looped over hooks, bosses or cleats make excellent tie-backs for curtains (see page 68). For a softer, prettier look, tie a generous bow in a sash of contrasting or matching fabric.

PERFECT PELMETS

Boxed In

If your instant curtain or blind is stapled to the windowframe, and you don't want to give the game away, you can hide the evidence with a pelmet (left). Corrugated card or packing material has a sculptural quality which is very appealing, and it is rigid enough to stretch across wide openings. Easily assembled, you need to construct a simple framework of battens to fit around the architrave – secure its joints with angle brackets and then nail into place. Cut the pelmet shape you want – make sure you leave enough card at each end to wrap around the batten framework at the sides. Glue in place the main pieces and decorate the front with curls of card (right).

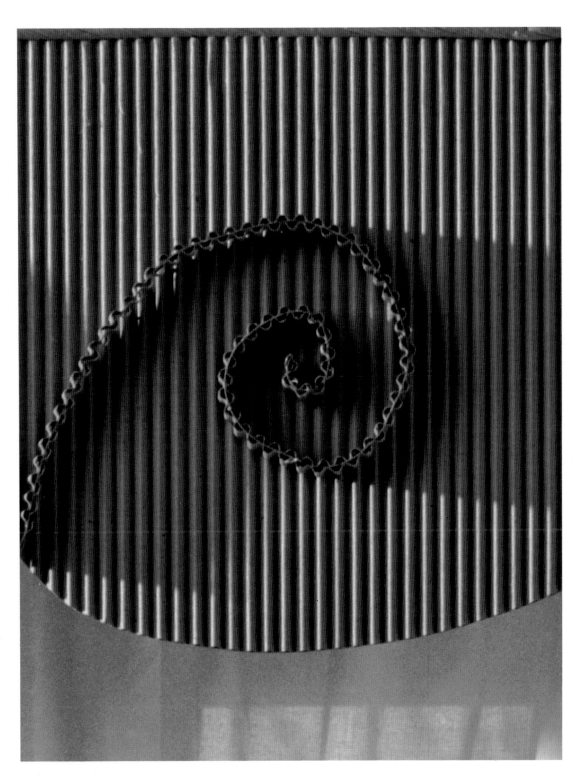

FRAMING THE VIEW

Pelmet Frame

The basic pelmet framework (right) **consists of lengths of 50×25mm (2×1in) stock cut to the required dimensions and joined at the corners with angle brackets. Angle brackets are also used to secure the pelmet to the wall. For extra rigidity, you could add short lengths of wood at each corner to support the edges.**

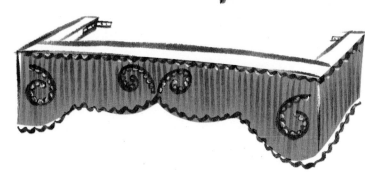

Paper Pelmet

Corrugated card makes a stylish choice for instant pelmets. Cut out the pelmet to fit and attach to the frame with glue. Decorate with cut swirls of card, or spray it gold (right).

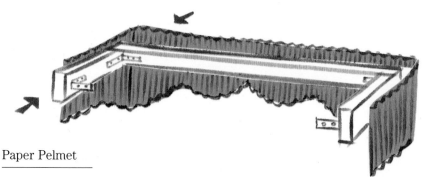

Over the Top

Use cardboard to imitate the extravagance of draped or carved pelmets. Cut two mirror-image shapes and stick to the pelmet frame with glue. Cover the central join with a shield shape and decorate it **with paint** (above and left).

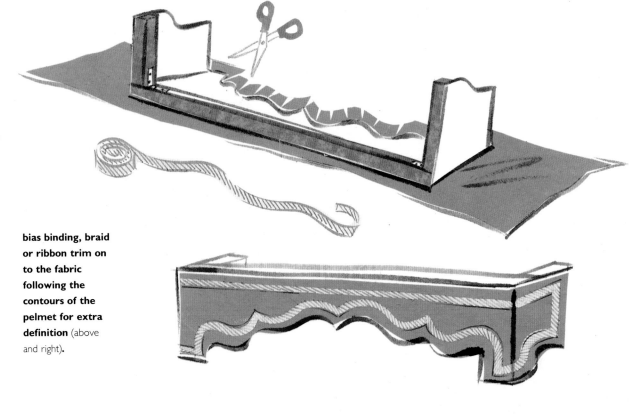

Fabric Covers

Basic card pelmets make a good base for covering with fabric. Simply wrap the material around the card and glue down edges. To cover intricate shapes, cut notches into the fabric edge to allow a neat turnover. Stick **bias binding, braid or ribbon trim on to the fabric following the contours of the pelmet for extra definition** (above and right).

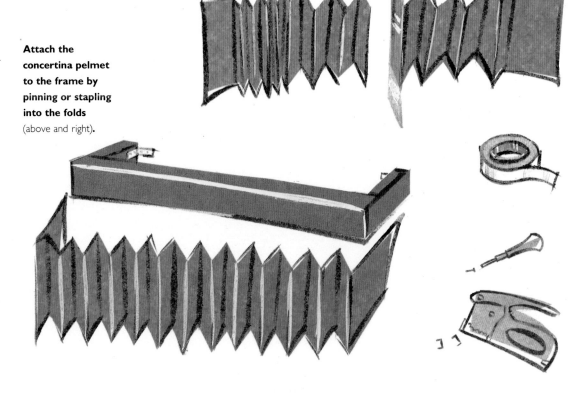

Concertina

For a sculptural effect, fold card into narrow folds. You will need to join pieces of card with double-sided sticky tape to make a concertina long enough to enclose the frame; and leave two flat side pieces at either end where the pelmet has to attach to the pelmet frame. **Attach the concertina pelmet to the frame by pinning or stapling into the folds** (above and right).

Driftwood

Natural inspiration was provided by this length of driftwood, utilized as a rustic curtain pole. Here, the driftwood is carefully balanced on long screws that have been driven partway into the wooden windowframe; alternatively you could attach a pair of cuphooks or screweyes to the underside of the window reveal and suspend the branch from those points. The hanging consists of eight squares of open-mesh dishcloths, stoutly tied and knotted together with short pieces of household twine.

No-sew Curtain

Nothing could be easier or more effective than this jaunty sweep of cotton thrown over a pole and gathered into a big knot at the level of the sill. Ensure that you buy enough fabric to extend right to the floor (left).

Tie-back

You can give the impression of luxuriously lined and finished drapery by tying a length of material in tight to make deep billowing folds. Here, rope wrapped neatly around a panel of hand-printed fabric makes a bold punctuation point (left).

Ribbons and Bows

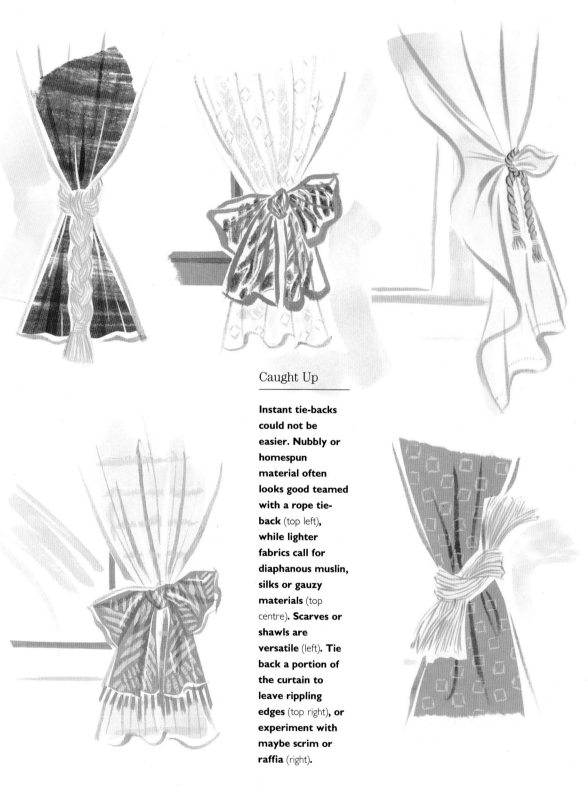

Caught Up

**Instant tie-backs
could not be
easier. Nubbly or
homespun
material often
looks good teamed
with a rope tie-
back** (top left)**,
while lighter
fabrics call for
diaphanous muslin,
silks or gauzy
materials** (top
centre)**. Scarves or
shawls are
versatile** (left)**. Tie
back a portion of
the curtain to
leave rippling
edges** (top right)**, or
experiment with
maybe scrim or
raffia** (right)**.**

No-sew Pelmet

**A fabric pelmet
can be created
with absolutely no
sewing. Allow
sufficient fabric to
gather softly
across the width of
the window. Apply
iron-on interfacing
to the reverse of
both top and
bottom edges,
turn over and
press in place.
Then cut vertical
slits about 4cm
(1½ inches) apart
across the width of
the pelmet at the
top and gather the
fabric along a wide
ribbon. The
curtain itself is
stapled or tacked
directly to the
windowframe.**

BLINDS

Awning

This improvised blind makes use of heavier-weight cotton in a broad stripe for the effect of an awning. Tacked in place along the top, long ties keep the neatly rolled lower edge in position. The crisp, striped design complements the checked sofa fabric and the cotton rug as well (left).

Tied Blind

Blinds are ideal for kitchen windows, as they can be pulled up well out of the way. This simple treatment combines the practicality of a blind with the softness of a curtain. Long tapes hold the folds in place (left).

Roller blinds in fabric, paper and cane are cheap and easy to install. They can also be decorated and trimmed in much the same way as fabric drapery or curtains (see page 58). You can also improvise blinds using material that is too lightweight for conventional roller blinds by rigging up a system of pull-up cords, tape or ribbon threaded through a pair of cup hooks. Alternatively, you can simply tie up the blind like a sail or awning and hold it in place using long tapes.

Although most people think in terms of fabric when it comes to covering windows, there are several other possibilities to consider which involve the use of different materials. If you do not need to worry about light control, but merely want to screen a view or gain a little privacy, you might consider filling the window embrasure with glass shelves to hold a collection of trailing plants, or lining up rows of coloured glass bottles and containers to make a jewel-like display against the light. You could even stand a screen so that it blocks the view from the lower half of the window but allows light to spill through into the room at the top.

FAST FURNISHING

Junk Shopping

Trimming

Most junk-shop finds need a little extra attention to bring them up to scratch. You can use upholstery trimming, such as this deep fringing, as a good way of disguising worn patches (left).

Check It Out

Ordinary kitchen chairs look great painted in a bright positive colour, and these flounced gingham skirts are easy to make. Attach iron-on interfacing to the top and bottom edges to make hems. Then cut vertical slits spaced about 4cm (1½ inches) apart and thread ribbon to gather the fabric up in pleats (far right).

Makeshift furniture is not merely for those short of cash. Even in quite well-heeled households there is often room for simple pieces rigged up with basic materials. One example is the cheap, circular, chipboard table, disguised with a floor-length skirt of fabric held in place with a round glass top. These little dressed tables, holding a lamp and collection of well-chosen objects in the living-room, or flanking the master bed, are something of a professional decorator's standby.

In the same spirit, you can make a kitchen dining-table from a flush door and a pair of trestles. Cover the door with oilcloth and staple it in place. If you need to increase the size of an existing table, borrow a trick often used in restaurants and rest a large circle cut from chipboard or block-board on top of the table, cover the board with felt and add a floor-length cloth to hide the deception.

If the idea of improvised furniture conjures up a depressing image of mattresses on the floor, milk-crate tables and scaffolding planks on bricks, think again. Such pitiful austerity is not the only alternative if the sofa of your dreams has a nightmare price tag or you'd need a second mortgage to buy a dining table and chairs. You can revamp old pieces with style, put a fresh face on tired tables and chairs and jazz up junk without descending to the level of the average student digs.

There is no escaping the fact that good-quality furniture, antique or new, will always cost money, but putting some of the ideas in this chapter into practice will prevent you from falling into the common trap of rushing out to buy a poorly made approximation of what you really want. If you buy something you don't like just because it is what you can afford, you will have to live with it while you wait for it to fall to pieces (as it almost certainly will). And the chances are that this will happen before you can afford to replace it with what you wanted in the first place. It is far better to apply lateral thinking to the whole problem, brush up your decorating skills, use your imagination and save up for the special sofa or bed.

JUNK SHOPPING

For basic tables and chairs, chests and even the odd sofa or bed frame, junk shopping remains a good strategy. You are more likely to find solid, decently made pieces at prices you can afford in markets, second-hand shops and salvage yards than in cut-price furnishing outlets. It is also well worth putting up with a little wear and tear for the sake of character.

Junk shopping makes economic sense as long as you know where to go and what to look for. Forget any notion that you may discover a priceless hoard

of antiques languishing in some dark corner of a dim, cobwebbed shop. The sophistication of the market, the proliferation of dealers and auction houses (some more scrupulous than others) and the eclectic nature of collecting today makes this an unlikely prospect. In the early part of this century, by contrast, the vogue was for furniture from the eighteenth and early nineteenth centuries. Victorian pieces, ignored and underrated, were therefore very well priced at that time. Nowadays, however, there is consistent demand for good pieces from all periods.

What does remain accessible is a plentiful supply of ordinary furniture (particularly from the 1930s onwards) that is practical, durable and often with at least some period charm. Poor finishes – stained, worn or discoloured can quickly and easily be covered up with a coat of paint. Shabby or stained upholstery can similarly be disguised under drapery if you can't afford recovering (see page 79). Look out for good, clean lines, intact, strong frames or carcasses, and sound springs and seats on upholstered pieces. Avoid wooden pieces with tell-tale pinholes that indicate worm – they may easily infect your other furniture.

It is a good idea to prepare yourself for forays into the second-hand field by doing a little basic research on furniture types and styles, as well as acquainting yourself with good markets, shops and auction houses specializing in the type of pieces you are looking for. Beware of impulse-buying and take dealers' claims with a generous pinch of salt. If you are unsure about whether or not to buy, a small deposit will usually secure an item while you think it over.

Architectural salvage yards and dealers in reclaimed shop fittings can also be a fruitful source. Old mahogany-and-glass shop-display units, plan chests from designers' or architects' offices and solid school cupboards are all good for storage purposes. Trunks, wicker laundry baskets, picnic hampers and banks of drawers originally used to house seeds, paints or ironmongery are equally versatile.

Dedicated urban scavengers who make a habit of scouring skips and building sites are constantly amazed at

the quality of materials and furniture other people seem happy to discard. If you are eagle-eyed and skilled at minor repairs you may find the odd treasure poking out from under a pile of builders' rubble. (But if there is any doubt about whether the piece has really been thrown out, be sure to ask permission before you haul it away!)

WRAPPING UP

Dressed Chairs

Two different styles for the same chair have been created with black curtain interlining, used matt-side-out and sprayed with large gold stars. The legs of one are wrapped in scrim sprayed gold; on both, the fabric is stapled in place to give neat edges (left).

It's a Wrap

Plain muslin dyed in brilliantly clashing pink and yellow has been bound around a simple wooden chair, covering the frame and seat completely (below).

Many sofas and chairs with good, clean lines, strong frames and a lot of life left in them are let down by shabby, stained coverings, which is not surprising as fabric wears out faster than wood. Unfortunately, loose covers elegantly tailored for a perfect fit or close-nailed upholstery with professionally piped seams demand the sort of skills which are not acquired overnight, and professional services tend to be expensive. While you are waiting for the cheque to come in, here are some solutions to tide you over.

Simplest of all is to drape the chair or sofa in a plain white cotton sheet (or you could dye the sheet in light, clear colours if you wanted). This tends to work best if more than one piece is draped – the look, of course, is the faded grandeur of out-of-season drawing rooms shrouded in dustsheets. Draping is also a good strategy in minimal surroundings in which you are aiming for a crisp, modern look. These instant covers can unify a disparate collection of furniture at little expense

and to dramatic effect. Again, as with window treatments, generous amounts of plain fabric suggests luxury; patterned or chintzy materials don't work in the same way. The special advantage of draping is that you can easily run the covers through the washing-machine when they start to look grubby.

Using the same principle, plain cotton can be tied or wrapped around basic kitchen chairs to give them enough style for formal dining. For a rococo effect, finish them with a sweeping bow at the back.

If you would prefer to use patterned fabric for your soft furnishings, it is generally more effective to layer different materials in sympathetic colours and designs. A single Indian bedspread thrown over a sofa – no matter how beautiful the pattern – is more reminiscent of the bedsit than the bazaar. But using the same fabric as a base and adding fringed paisley shawls, woven throws and cushions in complementary designs, you will achieve a rich tapestry of pattern that is far from forlorn.

Loose Covers

**Give a new lease
of life to old
armchairs by
improvising loose
coverings. Simple
disguise can be
very effective
when orginal
upholstery is worn
or discoloured**
(left)**. You don't
have to rely on
white sheeting for
instant cover-ups.
More exotic and
daring fabric
choices lend an air
of extravagance,
such as this
shimmering green
dress material**
(overleaf)**, also seen
draping french win-
dows on page 52.**

Decorative Finishes

Sitting Pretty

Cheap pieces of furniture can be made more cheerful with exuberant patterns painted on them. There is no need for restraint – going over the top by applying vibrant colour and design is much more effective than a half-hearted or hesitant approach. Oil-based paints are more durable, but emulsion simplifies the job and produces excellent results. A chair and table base break out in a rash of spots (left)**, while rush-bottomed country chairs are enlivened with a free-hand painted design** (right)**.**

The craze for stripping wood – particularly pine – has tended to obscure the potential of decorative furniture finishes. In the past, many pieces of everyday furniture were painted and enriched with patterns, often very colourfully. Such pieces were generally made of pine and other softwoods not considered fine enough to display in a more natural state. It was only furniture of higher quality, built in expensive mahogany, or veneered with exotic woods prized for the beauty of their figuring or their depth of colour, on which the wood was shown off. The modern obsession with stripping has revealed wood that was always intended to be covered up.

For the instant decorator, there is good historical precedent for painting furniture. It is also quick and easy to do. Commercial stripping, carried out in bulk by dipping pieces into caustic baths, can damage fine detail. The alternative, which is to strip the piece yourself, takes hours of diligent application with glasspaper, solvents and chemicals, taking off old layers of finish, filling cracks and then refinishing with wax, varnish or seal – a lot of bother if the wood was never supposed to be given this kind of exposure.

For colour and pattern inspiration, look at old cottage furniture, painted chalky blue or bottle green, or grained in attractive ochres and rich, smoky browns to give an impression of 'woodiness'. Then there are more exuberant examples in the folk-art idiom – the glowing reds and deep fir-greens of Scandinavian furniture; the bold stencilled designs of Americana; the singing cobalts and turquoises of the Mediterranean; and the clashing limes, oranges and pinks of Mexican decor.

WAYS WITH WOOD

More refined than rustic tables and chairs are historical pieces from the eighteenth and early nineteeth centuries. The spare lines of Neo-classical furniture were often complemented by subtle, light colouring: washed Gustavian blues and greys; pale straw or ivory highlighted with black lining and gilding. Regency chairs and tables were decorated in delicate eau-de-Nil, grey-green and gilt, or richly ebonized or lacquered in Chinese red.

Wooden furniture generally needs little in the way of preparation. A light sanding of gloss or varnished surfaces will ensure that fresh paint adheres properly. You can fill cracks and holes if you like, although this isn't necessary if you are aiming for a rustic look. Traditionalists recommend painting wood with oil-based paint, and for a single-colour treatment with a smooth finish, this is probably the best choice. Eggshell is subtler and less obvious than high-sheen gloss, which can look tacky and over-shiny. But water-based emulsion is the surprising choice of many contemporary furniture painters. Quick-drying and easy to use, emulsion covers well and provides a good surface for subsequent decoration, with the final finish much closer to the matt look of old painted pieces.

Painting not only freshens worn or discoloured finishes, but can serve to unify a disparate collection of country chairs or give an undistinguished table a jolt of style. Emphasize good lines by painting simple side-tables black for Hoffmann-style modernity, or decorate a set of children's chairs in different paintbox colours. You could also paint cupboards and chests to match the wall colour, increasing the sense of space in a room by simplifying the decoration

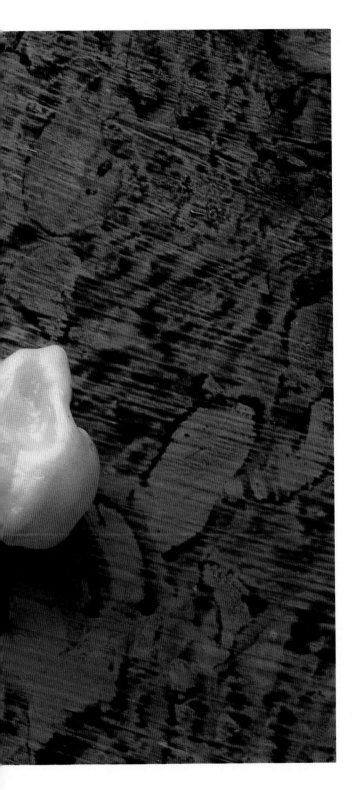

and making the furniture blend in with the walls. An 'unfitted' kitchen composed of dressers, cupboards and other free-standing pieces might benefit from this approach.

As with basic wall decoration, aged or distressed finishes can be more sympathetic and easier on the eye than glistening fresh paint. At its simplest, painted wooden furniture can be distressed merely by sanding back the paintwork along the edges and corners, where one would expect the finish to have worn. More elaborately, there are various recipes for crazed or crackled finishes if a more overt look of age is desired. You can also experiment with layers of different washes or glazes to build up the richness and depth of colour associated with the mellowing effects of time (see pages 26 and 27). Instant 'gilding' can simply be drawn in using metallic felt-tipped pens.

These distressed effects work well with other forms of painted decoration for a robust, farmhouse look. Stencilled or free-hand painted patterns can liven up drawer fronts, chair backs, bedheads and cupboard doors. Traditional motifs include flowers, garlands, hearts, stars and naive birds and animals. You can also add dates and initials.

Set off large motifs on panels and other flat surfaces with simpler borders on the legs or outlining the frames of a piece of furniture. Leaf shapes, spots, chevrons and rococo swirls emphasize the lines and generally add to the decorative exuberance. Don't be faint-hearted: less is not more when it comes to recreating traditions of folk decoration. Bright, dashing colours and layers of vibrant pattern express the powerful creative energies of these charming country styles.

Vinegar Graining

The traditional method of graining wood used a recipe containing stale ale. This modern update substitutes vinegar. First paint the surface with a coat of flat matt emulsion in a light colour: yellow works well grained with brown; for richer effects, try brick-red or grey-green grained in deeper tones of the same colour. Leave the paint to dry. Then make the graining glaze. Mix two tablespoons of vinegar with half a teaspoon of sugar and add powdered colour (brown, black, dark red or dark green) until the glaze runs freely. Brush on to the surface and then distress with a rolled-out piece of plasticine or putty, wiping off excess paint from time to time on to paper towels. Try out different directions to vary the pattern.

TOP TABLES

Patchwork Top

A junk table painted in a solid colour has a patchwork paper top assembled from torn scraps stuck down with wallpaper paste. When the paste has dried, seal the table top with a coat of clear matt varnish (below).

Instant Regency

Gold lines are drawn on a matt-black emulsioned surface with a felt pen to lend this simple table a sophisticated look. A whole star anise sprayed gold is a surprising substitute for a bronze mount (right).

Mosaic

A mosaic border encrusts a table top. Apply a layer of grout, thick enough to inset the mosaic, and colour the grout with a coat of emulsion. Press each piece in firmly and allow the grout to dry overnight (right).

SITTING PRETTY

Tartan Chairs

Sit down in style
on bold tartan
chairs. Paint a
base emulsion coat
and leave to dry.
Then build up a
plaid effect in
cross-hatched
stripes, using
sweeping confident
brushstrokes.
Don't worry if the
stripes are not
perfectly even –
imperfections are
a part of the
charm (left).

Checked Table

Apply a coat of
matt black
emulsion to legs
and base and
cover the top with
a coat of matt
white. The
checked finish is
determined by the
brush width. Use
a square-ended,
soft-bristled
watercolour brush.
Mix white and
black for a soft
mid-grey, and thin
with water for
transparency.
Paint grey stripes
over the white
base in one
direction, then
cross-hatch in
thinned black
paint. Wait for
each coat to dry
before going on to
the next (above).

NEW FROM OLD

An alternative to painted decoration is *découpage*. Despite the rather grand name, this technique involves nothing more elaborate than cutting out paper pictures and gluing them in place on to a wall or a piece of furniture. Wrapping-paper and greetings cards can be good sources of images to stick on a chair back or cupboard front. A coat of varnish will protect the paper cut-outs. *Découpage*, a favoured pastime of leisured Victorian ladies, often works best in a rather quaint idiom, featuring posies of flowers, cherubic children and garlands. You could also adapt the same technique and collage postcards or labels on to a table top for a more up-to-date look.

Still in the stick-on department, you can create patterns and borders three-dimensionally with a variety of customizing materials. Brass or metal upholstery nails can be used to edge drawer fronts or worked in repeating geometric designs, and are very effective on chests of drawers or trunk lids. Plain wooden moulding can be stuck on to cupboard doors to give the look of solid panelling in an instant. Even braid, gimp and ribbon can be stuck on as edgings for a decorative 'lift'.

Metal furniture offers its own decorative possibilities. The wonderfully evocative verdigris of old metal – the weathered, green-rust finish of park chairs and café tables exposed to the elements – is the height of current decorative fashion. But if real decay does not appeal to you, there are a number of excellent one-coat metal paints that will cover rusty surfaces with little or no preparation required. These are generally available in either metallic or flat colours and in textured or silky smooth finishes.

Collage Screen

Simple screens are
not hard to make
using precut
standard panels of
board secured
with screen hinges.
The fun begins
with decoration:
cover with fabric
or felt stapled in
place and trimmed
with glued-on
braid or ribbon;
spatter with flecks
of paint or stripe
with a cut roller;
or collage, as here,
with a vivid
patchwork of
patterned paper
which is sealed
with a coat of
clear matt varnish
to protect the
surface (left).

SCREEN TEST

Tartan Screen

Decorate a screen using cut-and-tied rollers to create a plaid paint effect (see page 24). The roller, instead of being cut into broad bands, was cut and tied into finer sections. A final coat of blue-tinted varnish softened the tones of paint (left).

Leaf Screen

This leaf screen features photocopied prints of an acanthus leaf. Two panels of the screen are covered in full A3 sheets, butted up. When stuck lengthways with wallpaper paste these exactly fill the width of our panel. The other two panels feature greater enlargements of the leaf for a more abstract effect. The screen was protected with acrylic varnish tinted with veridian green watercolour (right).

HIDING AWAY

Kitchen Tidy

Sunny checked washable fabric gathered on plastic-coated wire hides kitchen clutter from view, but allows easy access to shelves. A matching tablecloth helps to give coherence to a busy room (left).

Storage Units

Save old boxes, baskets and containers of every description to help ease storage problems in children's rooms and work areas. Shoe boxes can be given a new life covered in wrapping paper, and baskets can be painted to blend in or left plain (right).

Accessible, workable storage is essential to the running of any household, and it also keeps the emphasis where it belongs. If you want the elements of a room to work harmoniously and for displays to be effective, you need to eliminate clutter.

There never seems to be enough space for storage, even in the best-run households. Building in closets and cupboards is expensive and only worthwhile if you intend to stay in your home for a considerable time. It is often better and certainly cheaper, therefore, to exploit the versatility of containers to take the overflow.

Trunks, blanket-boxes and covered laundry baskets can hold a myriad of household items including toys, shoes, linen or magazines. Vegetable racks made of plastic-covered wire can be used for storing bathroom accessories, towels, stationery or nappies and changing equipment. Many DIY shops stock inexpensive sets of drawers in clear plastic or unfinished wood, for storing nails, screws and other hardware; you can put these to new uses storing spices, jewellery or cosmetics. In addition, a good supply of baskets always comes in handy in children's rooms, kitchens and bathrooms.

Painted garden trugs, orange boxes or fruit crates from the supermarket make virtually free storage boxes. Cheapest of all, cardboard hat- or shoe-boxes dressed up with wrapping-paper or fabric and neatly labelled provide an instant organization system for filing letters, bills, receipts and photographs. There's nothing new in this practice – bandboxes covered with leftover scraps of wallpaper provided a means of instant storage originally used in nineteenth-century America.

Hanging Space

Clothes left out hanging on a rail get dusty and fade in the sunlight; built-in wardrobes are expensive and traditional ones bulky. If you have an alcove to spare, beside a chimney breast for instance, this curtained hanging space provides a stylish solution, as well as protection for your clothes. Measure the width of the alcove and buy two expanding sprung metal rods of the correct length. Fit one inside the alcove as a clothes rail. Fit the second at the top, outside edge of the recess. Then hang doubled lengths of plain calico over the higher rod – as many as you need for the desired effect – and tie in front with raffia, scrim or ribbon. Alternatively, you can make rods from lengths of 5cm (2in) diameter wooden dowelling slotted into metal fittings.

BEDS

The bed was once the single most important piece of furniture in a household, handed down from generation to generation; in grand houses they were the focus of lavish expenditure on costly hangings and trimmings. Beds no longer hold such special significance but still have a vital role to play in our well-being and comfort.

When it comes to buying a mattress it is important never to cut corners. Cheap mattresses are a classic example of a false economy, and can harm your posture and lower your vitality. However, there are plenty of short-cut ways to trimming and furnishing a bed.

Enclosing a bed or bed alcove with fabric gives a suggestion of the grand beds of the past. Many of the ideas and fabrics suggested for the window drapery section, would work equally well as instant bed hangings, although you will need a framework from which to hang the drapery. A fine metal rod projecting out from the wall could take a sweep of light fabric to either side of a bed or you could attempt a basic wooden framework to decorate or drape as an instant four-poster.

Dressed Beds

**Fabric canopies
and hangings are
wonderfully
evocative and
romantic, and
make a refreshing
alternative to
thick bed curtains.
Billowing clouds of
muslin have been
dyed palest blue
and looped over a
simple frame,
tinging the early
morning light** (left).
**A filmy sari with
woven borders
makes a serene
canopy, draped
over a handmade
frame of metal
poles** (far left).

BED HANGINGS

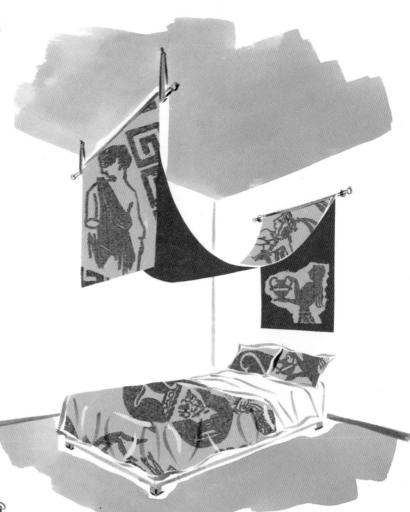

Canopy Bed

Drape a bed hanging overhead to create the effect of a canopy. Support a pole on two hooks screwed into the wall. Hang another pole from short lengths of rope or tape looped over another pair of hooks screwed into the ceiling at the bottom end of the bed (right).

Arabian Nights

A variation on the same theme, this delicate sari fabric is draped over poles held in place by pairs of metal pole holders attached to the wall behind the bed and to the ceiling (left).

Tester Bed

A picture frame is the basis for this grand effect (left). **Suspend the frame to the ceiling on short lengths of chain hung from stout hooks. Make sure that the hooks are screwed into the ceiling joists, not just into the plaster; check the position of joists by lifting floorboards in the attic or room above, or drill fine test holes in the ceiling. Staple a fabric pelmet and bed curtains to the inside of the frame.**

Four-poster

Lengths of bamboo or garden cane make a lightweight framework for filmy muslin or net drapery. Lash the canes together with stout twine or cord and suspend from the ceiling using butcher's hooks threaded through screw-eyes (right).

SWEET DREAMS

Picture This

The lightest fabric, which is often the most evocative and effective for such effects, needs very little in the way of support. A traditional picture hook clipped over

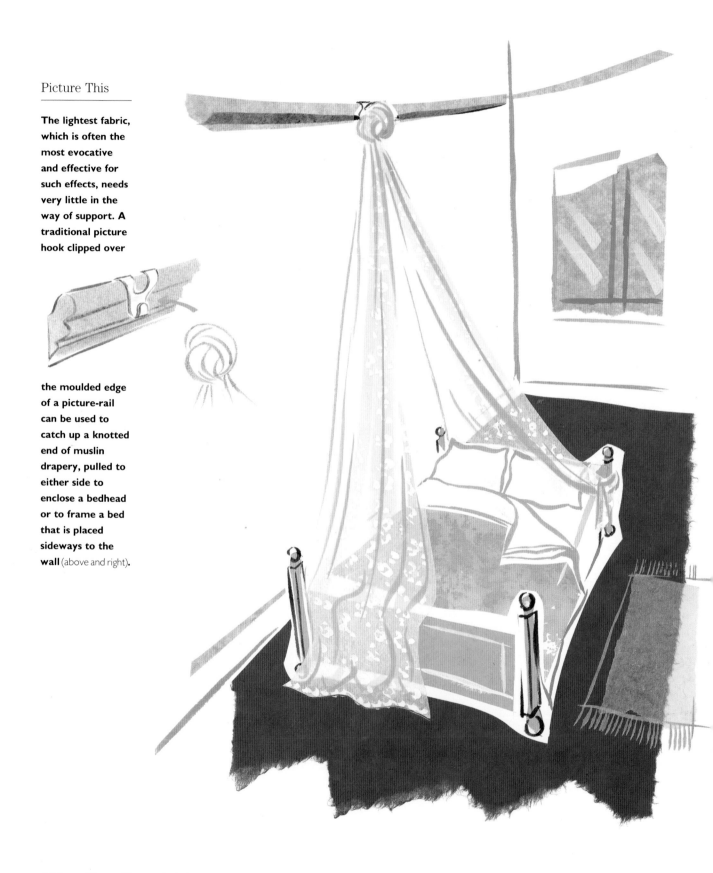

the moulded edge of a picture-rail can be used to catch up a knotted end of muslin drapery, pulled to either side to enclose a bedhead or to frame a bed that is placed sideways to the **wall** (above and right).

Mosquito Net

Borrow an idea from the tropics and screen the bed in fine netting. Wrap a metal hoop in net, sewing fabric tapes inside to keep the hoop in position. Then pull the top taut and knot in place. The netting can be drawn back and tied at either side (right).

Instant Bedhead

Pinch or sprung clips, usually available from upholsterers', are decorative in their own right and strong enough to support pillows or cushions on a pole for an instant bedhead (left).

SHOWING OFF

SHOWING OFF

The something-for-nothing approach to decorating really comes into its own when the issue is display. Pictures, treasures, mementoes – our lives would be immeasurably poorer if we were denied the opportunity to show off the things we enjoy and value. Displays are intriguing because they reveal individual tastes and interests; more than any other aspect of decoration, they lend warmth and personality. And because they can be changed frequently and readily, they are one of the best ways of creating a new look.

Showing off is not a question of displaying status. There is something deadening about a collection of perfect porcelain acquired for investment potential; what counts is not the value of the objects on show, but what they

More is More

The sheer density of collections is the secret of their appeal. A montage of precious family snapshots chronicles the years (above)**. Tin toys have a lasting attraction for the young at heart** (right)**. A tartan army of plates, cups and bowls multiplies the decorative impact of a basic design idea** (far right)**.

mean to you. Wit and humour can be particularly engaging, transforming the everyday by making you look at it afresh. Hats hung on the wall like trophies, kitchen paraphernalia in sculptural arrays or garish tin toys on the mantelpiece conjure visual magic out of the ordinary.

Even if what you put on view is no more functional than a piece of driftwood or a pile of beach stones, showing off can have its strategic uses. Clever arrangements draw the eye, directing the attention away from less-than-perfect skirting-boards, pock-marked walls and other imperfections. By inviting you to relish colour, texture or sheer eccentricity, this kind of decorative exuberance can help to make up for shortfalls in other areas.

RULES OF DISPLAY

Successful displays are all about creating impact. Scale, theme, positioning and lighting are aspects to consider, whatever you display.

Scale is one of the most important issues – and often the most neglected. A collection of small jugs dispersed around a room on various table tops, for example, contributes little decorative interest. The same collection, brought together in one place, 'reads' as a whole, immediately increasing the impact and attracting attention. Almost all collections owe a great deal of their appeal to the fact of being grouped, and it is this feature which deserves to be emphasized. By collecting objects or pictures in a group, you increase the scale of the display and prevent the fragmented look which results when things are just scattered randomly around the room.

When you collect objects together, you reveal their common denominator. You can have fun making up groups based around themes which appeal to you. Colour is an obvious link. Groups of similar objects in the same colour can be very powerful: rows of green plates on a dresser; blue glass jars on a window-sill; or white shells on a bathroom ledge. Equally, the theme of a collection could be type, material, texture, or origin. Victorian amateur naturalists prized their specimen cases of birds' eggs and butterfly wings; and today many people are intrigued by the graphic virtuosity of labels, packaging, matchboxes and other ephemera of consumerism. Remember that the point is not to aim for a collection of identical objects, but to create vitality and interest through diversity. Subtle variations on the theme – even the odd jarring contrast – will bring it all to life.

There are many natural locations for display. The mantelpiece lends itself to balanced symmetrical arrangements, while large objects can be grouped on the floor to one side of the hearth if the fireplace is not in use. Deep sills and window ledges are ideal for displaying glass or other materials which gain sparkle and intensity with light shining through them. Alcoves and corners can be fitted with shelves, and a deep rack or shelf at picture-rail height can be used to display a collection of plates, platters, dishes or jugs.

You don't have to be a museum or gallery curator to appreciate the importance of display lighting. All displays are enhanced by good lighting, natural as well as artificial. A table lamp will emphasize a tabletop collection; candlelight can add drama to a mantelpiece display. Mirror is an invaluable aid to spreading light, with objects ranged in front of it gaining the benefit mirror lends. Directional lighting can be angled to highlight a dresser packed with crockery, and a pendant lamp hung low over a dining-table will make an attractive pool of light over a centrepiece arrangement.

Shell Detail

Concave shells, such as these scallops attached to a mantlepiece, can also be used to adorn walls or chimney by filling the backs with quick-drying filler and then gluing them in place. Both the starfish and scallops shown here have been sprayed with gold paint and then slightly dulled with boot polish (left).

Grained Shelf

A simple shelf cut from man-made board has been given decorative lift: painted reddy brown and then mottled using black vinegar graining (see page 83), it forms the basis for a simple assembly of natural textures (below).

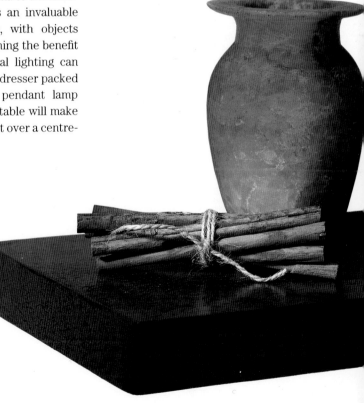

PRACTICAL PLEASURES

Everyday display makes a virtue of necessity, combining beauty with practicality. This is the charm of the *batterie de cuisine*, the hallstand, or the Shaker pegboard, where storage and display are combined.

The kitchen is an obvious location where usefulness is compatible with decorative interest. Kitchen utensils, have a special sculptural appeal hanging from hooks over a counter. A row of gleaming pots and pans is equally effective and instantly accessible on display, organized but good looking too. Jugs bristling with wooden spoons, open shelves of brightly labelled tins, and jars and bowls of fresh fruit and vegetables can form displays that marry efficiency with visual pleasure.

The appeal of the Shaker ethos rests on just this celebration of practical, well-made things. Shaker-style pegboards were originally used to suspend everything from chairs to brooms: what was not in active use was hung up out of the way in a simple yet systematic orderliness. For the like-minded, similar pegboards or rows of hooks can be adapted for displaying and tidying toys, clothes and bathroom accessories.

Bookshelves are another example of display storage. Books furnish a room, according to the saying; they convey warmth, liveliness and character. At the same time they are demanding in terms of space. Bookcases and shelving at the cheaper end of the market can be particularly unappealing, lacking all

style and distinction, but a few simple tricks can make the shelves look like they are part of the room rather than an afterthought. Wooden shelves, especially those built into alcoves, often look better painted the same colour as the main wall. You can glue a strip of moulding along the leading edge of each shelf to give the appearance of greater depth and solidity. Upholstery nails, fringing or the type of scalloped or toothed edging traditionally known as dust frills are other ways of dressing up plain shelves. Alternatively, you could wrap each shelf in fabric or felt, glued or stapled in place (see page 112). This type of upholstered look works well for shelves within display cupboards.

Open Shelves

Ordinary, every-day household objects don't need to be hidden away. Open shelves, especially in kitchens and eating areas, look both warm and hospitable. A rough-hewn dresser is trimmed with dried country branches (far left). Half-round sections cut from stout twigs and glued in place make corrugated edging for plain shelves (left).

Kitchen Ceramics

A collection of slipware provides colour and pattern inspiration for the free-hand decorative paint borders on this shelving unit built into a kitchen alcove (left).

CUPBOARD LOVE

Lining

The interiors of cupboards and dressers in constant use are seen as frequently as their exteriors. Make the view special by lining plain backs and shelves with fabric to complement the objects contained inside. Fold over the edges to prevent fraying, and stick in place using fabric glue (left). A revamped wall cupboard acts as a means of display for shells and other seaside treasures (above).

SHELVE IT

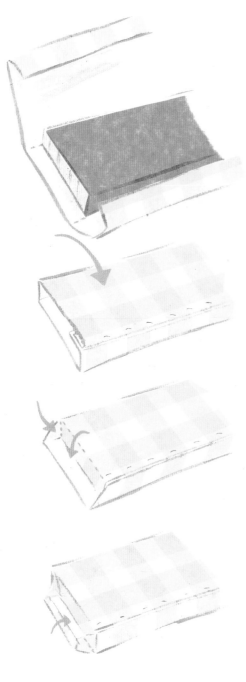

Wrapped Shelves

To completely enclose a shelf, turn up the back edge first and secure with glue, then bring the fabric round and fold over the top edge for a neat join. Secure with glue, pins or staples. Fold and mitre the corners just as if you were wrapping a gift (left). Alternatively, if the base of the shelf will not be on view you can leave the underside uncovered, as shown (right). Shelves *in situ* can be wrapped by attaching fabric first underneath at the back edge and then bringing the fabric round, and folding over the top edge for a neat, clean finish (below right).

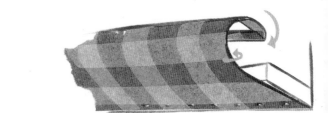

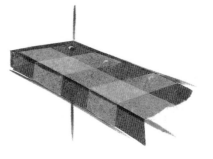

Lined Up

Wrapping adds instant style to uninspiring shelves and old storage boxes. Stripes, checks and other geometric prints lend a note of tailored distinction, complementing the rectilinear lines of shelving, but you will have to exercise some care to make sure all the edges and corners line up correctly (right).

NATURE'S WAY

Display Boxes

Small wooden drawers, printer's trays and cardboard boxes make ideal compartments for display. Place or glue treasures inside and hang the unit on the wall using either a ribbon or cord (above and right).

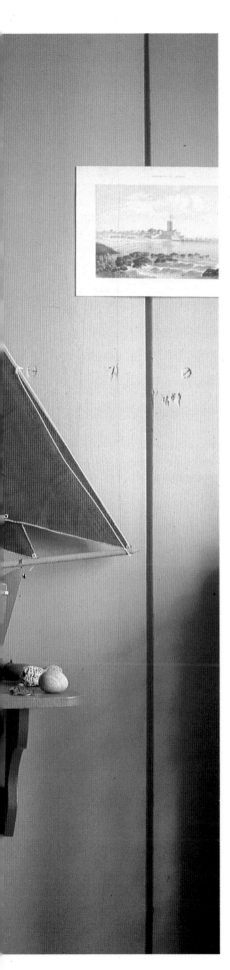

Themes

A hanging shelf carries a cargo of beach pebbles and a model yacht for an ocean-going theme (left). **Salvaged wood, worn by wind and water, is stuck straight on to the wall to frame fallen leaves** (right).

Cubbyholes

Wooden cubbyholes wrapped in newspaper make a textured display box. The open back is covered with scrim. Thinned water-based acrylic varnish, tinted a mahogany colour, is patchily absorbed by the paper (above).

PICTURES AND FRAMES

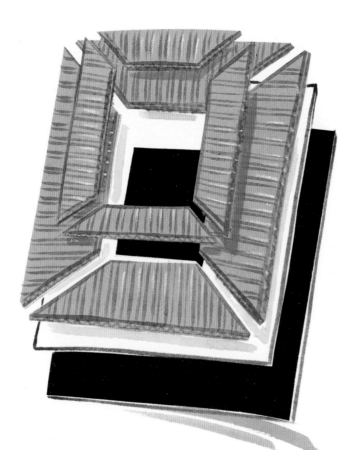

add an inner
frame, cut to half
the depth of the
base, and stick on
top to create the
effect of moulding.
The completed
frame can be
painted, sprayed
or decorated – but
looks equally good
left untouched (left
and below).

Card Frames

Rugged corrugated
paper makes
attractive and
robust frames for
snapshots and
postcards. First
make a base
frame from stiff
card to the
required
dimensions. Then
cut strips of
corrugated paper
to fit on top,
mitring the
corners. Finally

Variations

Different versions of the same paper frame can be made by adding cut-out shapes. As before, make a plain card base and then cut out a frame from corrugated paper to match, gluing it on top. Apply chunky squares at each corner (above) **or cut out circles to stick on top for a sculptural effect** (left).

The same general principles for displaying objects and collections also apply to picture-hanging. You can group similar types of work – black-and-white prints or photographs, watercolours, and so on – to increase their effectiveness, or assemble a collection of pictures related by theme, such as animal prints or images of food and drink for a kitchen.

When hanging a group of pictures, one useful tip is to lay them out on the floor or on a table top to experiment with positioning. Symmetry can be a good idea if all the pictures are the same size, although asymmetrical arrangement leaves open the possibility of adding to the collection at a later date. You don't have to restrict yourself to traditional locations, such as above the fireplace. Emphasize a doorway by hanging small prints to follow the outline of the architrave or run a low horizontal line of pictures over a sofa for Neo-classical elegance. Stairways and halls are good places for dense picture-hanging.

Original frames lift even the humblest photocopy out of the ordinary. Flea markets can be a good source of old, interesting frames, or you can decorate plain wood surrounds by painting or sticking on shells, stars, rope or fabric. One quick framing idea is to build up borders using layers of corrugated paper, either sprayed or left natural. Fabric tape, rope or ribbon are inventive ways of suspending pictures.

You can be just as eclectic in the selection of pictures you display. Prints of architectural detail, fresh from the photocopier, old photographs, collaged postcards, children's drawings – you don't have to patronize a gallery to find images that appeal to you.

FRAME IT

In The Frame

**Customize old
wooden frames
with paint, mosaic,
paper, stencilled
detail and fabric
bows. Then use
your imagination
about what you
put in the picture.
Paint offers many
possibilities: a
square-ended
brush dipped in
black makes a
checkerboard
pattern on an
ochre ground**
(above). **Or you can
cut a sponge into a
squiggle shape and
daub inky prints
on a warm, tinted
varnish base** (top
left, main picture).
**Stick on paste
jewels, or add**

bows of velvet, gauze or gingham as a finishing touch to a plain frame (main picture). **Torn scraps of paper can be pasted over a plain wooden frame** (right), **while anise stars, sprayed gold, trim the four corners of a matt-black frame** (below). **If you can't afford fine art, think laterally and display whatever catches your eye –** photocopied prints artificially aged in tea or washed with varnish,

sprayed leaves, pods and spices, shells, labels, fabric swatches and old family photographs can all form the basis for an imaginative and personalized picture collection.

LIGHTING

ighting is a vital element in the design of space and one of the key factors contributing to that indefinable sense of atmosphere which forms the basis of all successful decoration. Although you cannot radically alter lighting instantly, there are many ways of improving existing arrangements. Even on a tight budget there is a great deal you can do to create a better quality of light around the home.

Make a start by reviewing the colour and level of the light sources. Tungsten, the most common household light source, gives a warm yellowish light which is easy on the eye and flattering to skin tones. On the other hand, fluorescent strip lighting (often found in kitchens) is unpleasantly green in tone. Its pallid glare, responsible for the sickly look of many institutional buildings, can make people look distinctly ill. Getting rid of fluorescent lighting, particularly the overhead variety, will improve your decoration at once.

Any overhead light, especially if the bulb is bright, throws an even glare over the room, obliterating shadows, flattening shapes and minimizing textural variety. You can improve matters greatly by dispensing with central fixtures in favour of individual points of light from table lamps or spotlights. These create atmospheric pools of light and shade, throw detail into relief and are every bit as effective in practical terms. And for economical, no-nonsense lighting it is hard to beat those versatile modern classics, the anglepoise lamp and the clip-on loft light, both stylish enough for living-rooms, and also suitable for other lighting applications in the home.

There is a wide range of affordable lamps on the market, with plain cer-

amic bases in uncontroversial shapes and colours. Needless to say, these can be customized easily by sticking on stars, sequins or anything that adds a little extra glitter and glamour. Lamp bases can also be painted to fit in with your overall colour scheme or to stand out as a splash of interest. You can paint them using emulsion or enamel paints, or you could use special ceramic

paints available from artists' suppliers. These are extremely easy to use and are 'fired' in an ordinary oven, but do note that such paints should never be used on plates or other items intended for food use. Plain shades can also be decorated with paint, ribbon or trimming, covered with patterned paper or fabric, or collaged with any number of natural 'found' materials.

Striped Shade

Revamp a plain fabric lampshade with painted stripes (left). **Trace around the outer and inner circumferences of the shade, marking the seam where the fabric joins. Divide the circles into sixteenths (less or more depending on how wide you want the stripes). Cut out the inner circle and place it on top of the shade, aligning one of the marked points with the seam; then place the bottom of the shade on top of the outer circle, again aligning one point with the seam. Next, transfer the marked points back on to the shade. Apply masking tape as shown, and then paint alternate segments in a contrasting colour. When the paint is dry, remove the masking tape.**

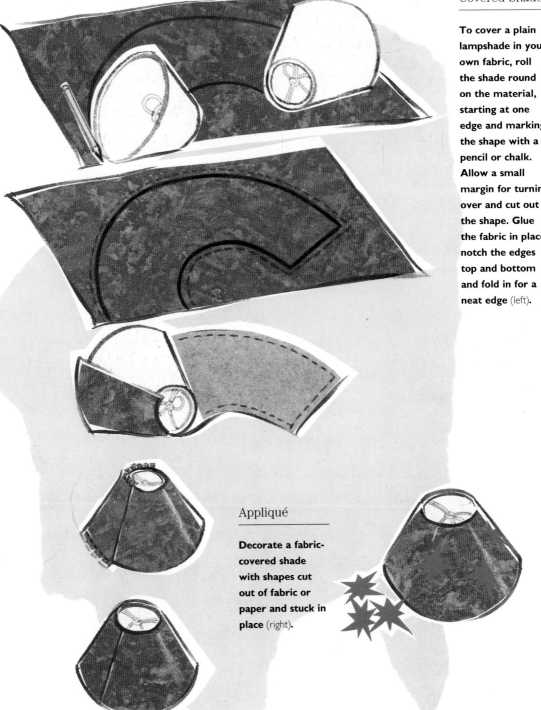

Covered Shade

To cover a plain lampshade in your own fabric, roll the shade round on the material, starting at one edge and marking the shape with a pencil or chalk. **Allow a small margin for turning over and cut out the shape. Glue the fabric in place, notch the edges top and bottom and fold in for a neat edge** (left).

Appliqué

Decorate a fabric-covered shade with shapes cut out of fabric or paper and stuck in place (right).

FLOWERS AND PLANTS

Containers

Hot Mexican colours transform garden plant pots into stylish containers for a collection of bristly cacti (left). **Fragile sweetpea flowers in plain glass containers, set on a sunny window-sill form a bold but simple display in an instant** (right).

Canny retailers know that the tantalizing aroma of coffee or the smell of baking bread can stimulate well-being and free-spending in their customers. Students of the property market advise that soft background music and fresh flowers in every room clinch more deals than the most fulsome agent's prose. Such seemingly intangible factors play at subtle unconscious levels and greatly contribute to the overall sense of place.

Flowers bring life to the most clinical of surroundings. We instinctively appreciate some symbolic link with nature, even if it is just a straggling pot plant or a jug of spring daffodils. If you apply basic design sense in this area, too, you can make flowers and plants a more positive element in decoration.

As with any kind of display, scale is important. If fresh flowers represent a luxury item in your weekly budget, it is better to invest in a greater quantity of cheap flowers (generally those in season) which will have more impact than a few select blooms. Reflecting seasonal change through your choice of flowers is also a good way of bringing a sense of the outdoors closer to home.

Unless you have a well-stocked garden, free flowers mean wild-flowers which should be left alone to flourish. One exception is the hardy flowering species known as cow parsley (Queen Anne's lace), which is rampant in summer on wayside verges and wasteground. The delicate white and fresh green of these flowers make excellent countrified arrangements, either on their own or combined with a few bought flowers. If you do have a garden, raid it regularly not just for flowers, but for foliage, berries, autumn leaves and bare winter branches to supplement more traditional arrangements.

Containers for displays could not be easier to improvise. While a selection of jugs, vases and plain glass containers are useful, galvanized pails, watering cans, jam-jars tucked inside baskets and even test-tubes have all been used

to great effect by the more original floral designers. What counts is matching the style of the container to the quality of the flowers or foliage on display: delicate stems and fragile blooms in glass containers, spring bulbs in baskets or terracotta pots, robust country bouquets spilling out of earthenware or enamelled jugs.

Houseplants (as opposed to displays of cut flowers, foliage or branches) have fallen from favour in fashionable circles in recent years. But whatever high style may decree, growing plants in containers will always be a satisfying and popular way of appropriating nature. The domestic charm of a row of bright geraniums on a sunny kitchen window-sill, the dense tangle of fern fronds on a steamy bathroom ledge, or the dark trails of ivy tumbling over the side of a dresser will never disappoint. Truly exotic plants, such as succulents and cacti, are fascinatingly ugly, while herbs grown in containers are practical as well as beautiful.

Houseplants are best grouped together in locations which serve their needs. There are usually only a few sites around the home which can support plant life well, where light and warmth or moisture and shade are optimum for a particular family of plants. Happily, the needs of design and nature coincide: where conditions are right, fill the area with plants to make an impressive display. Stagger heights by combining hanging plants with plants on stands and at floor level. It is worth taking the time and trouble to decant plants from plastic pots into terracota ones, which can easily be 'aged' by rubbing them with a little live yoghurt or unpasteurized milk to encourage the growth of lichen.

INDEX

ACKNOWLEDGMENTS

The publisher would like to thank the following photographers and organizations for their permission to reproduce the photographs in this book:

6–7 Tim Street-Porter/Elizabeth Whiting and Associates; **8–10** above Tim Street-Porter; 10 below Roland Beaufre/Agence Top; **11** IPC Magazines/Robert Harding and Associates; **12–13** Margaret Courtney-Clarke; **14–15** Stylograph/Bayo; **16–17** ESTO/Mark Darley; **18** above IPC Magazines/Robert Harding Picture Library; **18** below Paul Ryan; **18–19** IPC Magazines/Robert Harding Picture Library; **20** Paul Ryan; **20–1** David Brittain/Metropolitan Home; **22** above Stylograph/P.Isla/Casa de Marie Claire; **23** left Fritz von der Schulenburg (Richard Hudson); **23** right Peter Woloszynski/Elizabeth Whiting and Associates; **29** Bruant/Puech/Postic/Marie Claire Maison; **30–1** Chabaneix/Bayle/Marie Claire Maison; **31** right Shona Wood (designer: Georgina Godley); **36** Michael Dunne/Elizabeth Whiting and Associates; **37** right Bailhache/Comte/Marie Claire Maison; **37** left Hussenot/Roy/Comte/Marie Claire Maison; **38** IPC Magazines/Robert Harding Picture Library; **39** left Stylograph/Olivier de Lerins/Côté Sud; **39** right Tim Street-Porter/Elizabeth Whiting and Associates; **40** Chabaneix/Bastit/Maire Claire Idées; **41** IPC Magazines/Robert Harding Picture Library; **42** left Camera Press; **42** right Ianthe Ruthven; **46–7** Stylograph/Ingalill Snitt/Côté Sud; **48–9** Roland Beaufre/Agence Top; **50–1** IPC Magazines/Robert Harding Picture Library; **55** IPC Magazines/Robert Harding Picture Library; **58–9** IPC Magazines/Robert Harding Picture Library; **66** Jean-Pierre Godeaut; **67** Christian Sarramon; **70** Christian Sarramon; **71** IPC Magazines/Robert Harding Picture Library; **72–3** Stylograph/Samcassani; **74** IPC Magazines/Robert Harding Picture Library; **77** Christian Sarramon; **80** Di Lewis/Elizabeth Whiting and Associates; **81** Christian Sarramon; **88–9** Chabaneix/Marie Claire Idées; **92** Nadia Mackenzie; **93** IPC Magazines/Robert Harding Picture Library; **96** left Victor Watts/Elizabeth Whiting and Associates; **96–7** Chabaneix/Chabaneix/Bastit/Marie Claire Idées; **102–3** IPC Magazines/Robert Harding Picture Library; **104** left Chabaneix/Bayle/Marie Claire Maison; **104–5** Nadia Mackenzie; **105** right Camera Press; **108** left Stylograph/B.Touillon/Côté Sud; **108** right Morel/Puech/Marie Claire Maison; **109** Chabaneix/Chabaneix/Bastit/Marie Claire Idées; **110** Stylograph/B.Touillon/Côté Sud; **111** IPC Magazines/Robert Harding Picture Library; **114** above left Camera Press; **114–5** Gilles Guerin/Agence Top; **124** Nadia Mackenzie; **125** Di Lewis/Elizabeth Whiting and Associates.

SPECIAL PROJECTS
The projects on the following pages were devised and specially photographed for Conran Octopus: 2, 4–5, 22 below, 24–5, 28, 32–3, 43, 52–3, 54, 57, 60–1, 64–5, 68–9, 75, 76, 78–9, 82–3, 84–5, 86–7, 90–1, 94–5, 106–7, 113, 114 below left, 115 right, 118–9, 122–3.

Art Direction *Claire Lloyd*
Photography *Richard Foster*
Photographic Assistant *Hannah Lewis*
Art Director's Assistant *Tiffany Davies*
Set Building *Jon Self*

BRAZIL

Brian Dicks

Evans

TITLES IN THE COUNTRIES OF THE WORLD SERIES:
BRAZIL • FRANCE • JAPAN • KENYA • UNITED KINGDOM • USA

Published by Evans Brothers Limited
2A Portman Mansions
Chiltern Street
London W1U 6NR

VISIT OUR WEBSITE
www.evansbooks.co.uk
Evans

Produced for Evans Brothers Limited by
Monkey Puzzle Media Limited
Gissing's Farm, Fressingfield
Suffolk IP21 5SH

First published 2002
© copyright Evans Brothers 2002
© copyright in the text Brian Dicks 2002

British Library Cataloguing in Publication Data
Dicks, Brian
Brazil. - (Countries of the world)
1.Brazil - Juvenile literature
I.Title
981

ISBN 0 237 52270 5

Editor: Polly Goodman
Designer: Jane Hawkins
Map artwork by Peter Bull
Charts and graph artwork by Encompass Graphics Ltd
All photographs are by Edward Parker except: *Corbis Digital Stock* Imprint & Contents, 17, 61; Popperfoto 39 (STR/Reuters).

Endpapers (front): São Paulo, Brazil's largest city and the third-largest city in the world.
Title page: The towns of Olinda and, in the background, Recife.
Imprint and Contents page: The Iguaçu Falls, one of the natural wonders of the world.
Endpapers (back): A fishing trip in Amazonia.

The Brazilian flag. The green and yellow colours stand for forests and minerals. The blue sphere bears the motto *Ordem e progressso* meaning 'Order and Progress'. The 27 stars, arranged in the pattern of the night sky over Rio de Janeiro, represent Brazil's states and federal district.

Large areas of Brazil are wilderness: rugged, forested, isolated and little explored.

B razil is the world's fifth-largest country in both area and population. It is also the largest country in South America, covering some 47 per cent of the continent's area with over 51 per cent of its population. Only Russia, Canada, China and the USA (including Alaska and Hawaii) are greater in area. Brazil shares borders with all South American countries except Chile and Ecuador.

At its widest point, the distance from west to east across Brazil is over 5,000km, greater than the distance between London and Moscow. Even greater is the distance from its most northern to its most southern points, between the Guyana border in the north and the south-west border with Uruguay, which is roughly 6,000km. Brazil is so big there are three different time zones across the country, varying between 3–5 hours behind GMT. It is little wonder, therefore, that Brazilians say they live in a 'continent' rather than a 'country'.

A COUNTRY OF EXCESSES

With its huge land size and population, Brazil is a country of excesses. It has the world's largest rain forest and the mightiest river

KEY DATA

Area:	8,547,404km²
Highest Point:	Pico da Neblina (3,014m)
Population:	170.1million (2000)
GDP per Capita:	US$7,037*
Currency:	Real
Capital City:	Brasília

Major Cities: (population 1999)

São Paulo	(16.6 million)
Rio de Janeiro	(10.3 million)
Belo Horizonte	(4.6 million)
Salvador	(3.1 million)
Fortaleza	(2.3 million)
Language:	Portuguese

* Calculated on Purchasing Power Parity basis
Sources: UN Population Division; World Bank; *Der Fischer Weltalmanach 2001, Frankfurt am Main*

system. Its mountains and plateau areas contain some of the world's biggest reserves of industrial and precious minerals and it has the world's largest hydroelectric power (HEP) station. It exports more coffee and sugar than any other country. Brazil's Atlantic coast stretches some 7,400km, the longest continuous coastline of any country. It has the world's largest football stadiums, the most exotic street carnivals and some of the biggest cities. With its size and resources, Brazil is the giant of South America.

A DIVERSE COUNTRY

Brazil is a diverse country in both landscapes and people. Its population is one of the most varied in the world, a mixture of many cultures from all the continents. Its economy is developing fast, the fastest of South America, and Brazil is now the 49th-richest country in the world. Yet many Brazilians live in extreme poverty and there is a great gap between rich and poor. Despite being the wealthiest South American country, Brazil has an enormous foreign debt, has experienced

Brazil has the fifth-largest population in the world, with over two-thirds of its people under the age of 30 years.

periods of crippling inflation and has major problems of social and economic inequality, illiteracy, pollution and crime.

Yet despite the great gulf between extreme wealth and grinding poverty, in both the cities and the countryside, Brazilians are extremely proud of their country, which manages to function as 'one nation', drawn together by language and culture. At carnival and football games, all Brazilians are equal!

São Paulo is Brazil's largest city and the third-largest city in the world.

CASE STUDY
PORTUGUESE COLONISATION

During the 'Great Age of Discovery', in the late fifteenth century, Spain and Portugal wanted to extend their empires into the Americas. In 1494, the Treaty of Tordesillas divided South America between Portugal and Spain. But the pattern of exploration led to Portugal gaining much more land than the treaty specified. Among the earliest Portuguese sea captains was Pedro Alvares Cabral, who investigated the coasts around Rio de Janeiro (see page 44). Further discoveries followed so that by the end of the sixteenth century almost half of South America had been claimed as a Portuguese colony. It was ruled by a governor-general from Salvador, Brazil's first capital. In 1889, Brazil severed its political links with Portugal and declared itself a republic.

Much of the Amazon basin is flooded in the wet season, from January to June each year.

STATES AND REGIONS

Brazil's official name is *República Federativa do Brasil* (Federal Republic of Brazil). Its capital is Brasília. The huge country is divided into 26 states and a federal district. The federal district is Brasília, the newly planned city that succeeded Rio de Janeiro as Brazil's capital on 21 April 1960.

Each state has its own capital city, governor and parliament. The states are largely self-governing, except where issues of national concern are involved, such as defence, currency and foreign relations. They are controlled by the federal government, headed by an elected president. Between 1964 and 1985, five Brazilian presidents were military leaders who resorted to dictatorship rather than democracy. A new constitution came into force in 1988, with a return to democracy in 1990.

THE REGIONS

As well as its states, Brazil is divided into five large regions. Formed out of groups of states, the regional boundaries are used for administrative and statistical purposes and to help the country's general strategic planning. The regions vary in area and population, and have different landscapes, histories and modern issues.

THE NORTH

Most of this region lies within the Amazon basin and is covered by tropical rain forest. Its main issue is environmental protection from uncontrolled economic development.

THE NORTHEAST

The Northeast was Brazil's first area of colonial settlement and it has the most colourful mix of cultures, including strong African influences. The area has crippling poverty and unemployment.

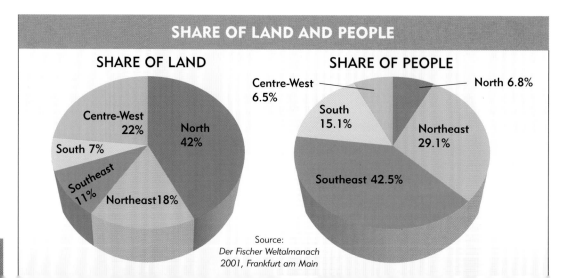

SHARE OF LAND AND PEOPLE

SHARE OF LAND

Centre-West 22%
North 42%
South 7%
Southeast 11%
Northeast 18%

SHARE OF PEOPLE

Centre-West 6.5%
North 6.8%
South 15.1%
Northeast 29.1%
Southeast 42.5%

Source:
Der Fischer Weltalmanach 2001, Frankfurt am Main

THE SOUTHEAST

This is Brazil's economic powerhouse and home to almost half its population. The region's wealth attracts migrants to its large cities, especially São Paulo, Rio de Janeiro and Belo Horizonte.

THE SOUTH

The South is another highly developed region with a more temperate climate than the North. It has attracted immigrants from Germany, Italy and other European countries, whose descendants have kept their languages and customs alive.

THE CENTRE-WEST

Until the 1940s, this region was one of the last great, unexplored areas on earth. Although home to the country's capital Brasília, the Centre-West remains largely undeveloped.

Santos is Brazil's major port, in the prosperous Southeast region.

In northern Brazil, people live in scattered groups throughout the Amazon rain forest.

Only China, India, the USA and Indonesia have larger populations than Brazil. In 2000, the population was 170.1 million, which gave an average population density of just 202 Brazilians living in every square kilometre. But there are great differences in the population density around the country.

POPULATION DISTRIBUTION

Large areas of Brazil have very few people, and some have no people at all. These sparsely populated areas contrast with the immensely overcrowded cities, especially in

Curitiba, in the South, is a densely populated city, a magnet to migrants from poorer parts of Brazil.

the Southeast, where official figures are under-estimates and densities can only be guesses. These variations in population distribution are the result of factors such as accessibility, topography, the climate, the availability of mineral and farming resources and, importantly, the history of colonialism and settlement.

The population density map (see page 13) shows a fairly simple pattern. Over 90 per cent of Brazilians live in a zone along the Atlantic coast, which stretches inland for up to 500km. These coastal areas were the first to be colonised by Portuguese and other Europeans from the sixteenth century, and they have kept their economic and political importance to this day. Together, the Southeast and South regions are home to 57.6 per cent of Brazilians, whereas the North and Centre-West, the country's two largest regions by area, contain only 13.3 per cent of the population.

Population density
(number of persons per km^2)

More than 23

10–23

1–10

Less than 1

● Cities and conurbations with over 1 million people

POPULATION GROWTH

Brazil's population has trebled over the last fifty years (see graph). This growth is due to two processes: natural increase and large-scale immigration. However, the rate of increase has been slowing down, from 2.8 per cent a year in the 1960s to 1.7 per cent in the late 1990s. This is the result of social changes, which are leading to smaller families. Brazil is a Roman Catholic country, where contraception is not widely practised and abortion is illegal. However, abortion is frequently resorted to, with estimates of 3–6 million abortions a year. Also, about 30 per cent of Brazilian women of child-bearing age have been sterilised.

POPULATION STRUCTURE

Brazil is a young nation, with the 'bottom-heavy' population structure of a Lesser Economically Developed Country (LEDC). Seventy per cent of Brazilians are under 30 years old and one-third are under 15. This means that there is enormous pressure for jobs, new schools and welfare services. The present population growth means that some 1.5 million new jobs are needed every year. The proportion of over 65s is only 3 per cent compared with 13 per cent for Germany and other Western economies. The small number of old people shows the need for health improvements to increase people's life expectancy.

POPULATION GROWTH

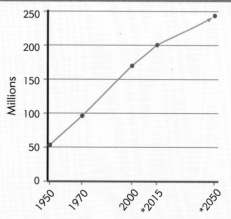

Sources: UN Population Division; *Geographical Digest*; UNDP   *=Estimates

POPULATION STRUCTURE

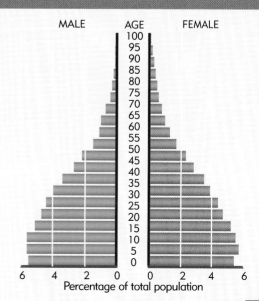

Source: *Understanding Global Issues: Brazil* (UGI Ltd, 1999)

Rain-forest peoples still collect the red dye from the brasilwood tree, the tree that gave Brazil its name.

THE FIRST BRAZILIANS

The first people of Brazil were the Amerindians, who have lived on the continent for thousands of years. Unlike the Spanish *conquistadors* (conquerors) of the early sixteenth century, who discovered advanced native civilisations in Peru and Mexico, the Portuguese settlers of the early 1500s found far less sophisticated peoples when they

CASE STUDY
TERRA DO BRASIL

Early Portuguese traders named Brazil after the brasilwood tree, which can be used to produce a red dye. The Amerindians had long used the tree and its dye for many purposes, especially for painting their bodies. The Portuguese collected the wood and shipped its pulp to Europe, but the trade failed to lead to much success. However, it did give Brazil its name. *Brasa* in Portuguese means 'embers' or 'glowing coals', referring to the redness of the wood. Soon the colony was known as '*terra do brasil*', meaning 'land of the red dye-wood'.

arrived in Brazil. The most advanced group were the Tupi Guarani, who lived in large coastal and riverbank villages growing manioc (cassava) and other crops, hunting, fishing and gathering fruits. But the Tupi Guarani had no stone buildings, no metal implements and only a basic administrative system. Inland from the coast other Amerindian peoples existed essentially as hunters and gatherers.

When the Portuguese arrived, in the early 1500s, the number of native Amerindians in what is now Brazil was probably around 8 million, but away from the rich food supplies of the coast their densities were low. The colonists used the Amerindians as slaves. Others were killed by adventurers as they searched for gold, valuable wood and other riches. Many other Amerindians died from exposure to European infectious diseases, to which they were not immune.

Many Portuguese took Amerindian wives, which was the start of the process of miscegeneration (the interbreeding of races) which has created such a diverse range of peoples in Brazil. Today there are probably around 200,000 Amerindians left in Brazil, and they are still under threat from developers. A number of organisations are campaigning for the protection of Amerindian land and cultural rights.

A MULTICULTURAL SOCIETY

Brazil's population is often described as a 'melting pot' – 'always simmering and sometimes reaching boiling point'. Brazilians are a mixture of many different races, including native Amerindians, European colonists, Africans and other immigrants. Between the sixteenth and nineteenth centuries, the Portuguese shipped millions of African slaves from West Africa to Brazil, to work on their large plantations. Around 10 million arrived in Brazil before slavery was finally abolished in 1888. Their descendants are an important element in modern Brazil's colourful mix of peoples, especially in the state of Bahia, often called 'Africa in exile'.

Not surprisingly, a large proportion of Brazilians are of Portuguese origin, but there are also large numbers of Italians, Spanish, Germans, Poles, Japanese and, more recently, Koreans and Middle Easterners, who have come to Brazil. To these immigrants Brazil was, and still is, a 'land of opportunity'.

Pure Amerindians make up less than one per cent of the population. A larger proportion is made up of the *mamelucos*, the descendants of white Europeans and Amerindians. Other racial groups are the *cafuso* (those of Amerindian and African descent) and the *mulatto*, those of black and white descent.

The government's official view is that racial intolerance does not exist in Brazil. Many argue, however, that it is as deep-rooted as in parts of the USA and South Africa. 'The whiter you are the richer you are' is a common Brazilian saying. Without doubt, the poorest rural and urban communities are the black *mulatto* and *cafuso*.

ABOVE: The Northeast was the heart of the African slave trade, a legacy left in the region's people and culture. This Bahian woman is dressed in traditional costume.

BELOW: Nineteenth-century immigration has given the South a distinctive European flavour, as shown in the architecture of the town of Blumenau, which has a strong German feel.

The rolling expanse of Mato Grosso state in the Brazilian Highlands.

Brazil can be divided into five main physical regions. In the north, the wild Guiana Highlands are shared with Venezuela, Guyana, Surinam and French Guiana. The highest mountain is Pico da Neblina (3,014m), near the Venezuelan border. The Guiana Highlands are the source of many large south-flowing tributaries of the Amazon river system, and of others flowing north to Venezuela's Orinoco river.

The Brazilian Highlands, in the centre of the country, form an enormous plateau of between 200–2,000m in height, with abrupt escarpment edges and several higher mountain ranges. They form a huge watershed between the large, north-flowing Amazon tributaries and the tributaries of the Paraná and Paraguay rivers. These river valleys slice through the plateau to form well-defined tablelands, called *chapadas*. Many impressive waterfalls occur along their steep edges. An important river that is confined to the Brazilian Highlands is the São Francisco. Starting in the state of Minas Gerais, it flows north before turning east to meet the Atlantic.

Between the Guiana Highlands and the Brazilian Highlands is the Amazon basin. Here, a vast lowland covered by rain forest stretches from the Andean foothills to the Atlantic. In the far west the lowland is 1,300km from north to south, but it narrows considerably eastwards where the Guiana and Brazilian Highlands are closer together. The Amazon basin is a vast drainage system feeding the mighty Amazon river. It is four times larger than that of Africa's Zaire river, and eleven times larger than the Mississippi drainage basin in the USA. Of the world's largest rivers, ten are in the Amazon basin.

Brazil's other main lowland area is much smaller than Amazonia, but still large by European standards. It shares part of the flat upper Paraguay basin with Bolivia and Paraguay. This is now the Pantanal Wildlife Reserve (see page 21) which, with an area of 230,000km^2, is about the size of the UK.

The country's coastal belt, which stretches for over 7,400km, is bordered by the Atlantic and the eastern edge of the Brazilian Highlands. Mountainsides drop steeply to the sea, especially along the Great Escarpment, which extends from Pôrto Alegre to Salvador. The coastal belt is made up of pockets of lowland, many with natural harbours, which were important to the early settlement and economic development of Brazil.

…ese spectacular waterfalls are on the border ´ Brazil and north-eastern Argentina, and ·km from the Paraguay border. The Iguaçu …er begins near Curitiba, very close to the …lantic. As it flows westwards, it is fed by ·out 30 tributaries, before spectacularly …unging 80m down a crescent-shaped cliff. …e waterfalls are one of the scenic wonders ´ South America, and a major Brazilian …urist site. At times of peak flow, the water …mbles over 275 falls and cascades, with …ough volume to fill six Olympic-sized …vimming pools every second. But in some …ars rainfall is so slight that the river dries up …ogether, as it did in May and June 1978.

The Iguaçu Falls are one of Brazil's main tourist attractions. They are also listed as one of the seven natural wonders of the world.

LANDSCAPE FEATURES

Fishermen with their traditional sailing boats, or *jangadas*, on the white sands of the tropical Northeast.

CLIMATE AND WATER RESOURCES

Brazil has a mostly warm and humid tropical climate, due to its position close to the Equator. In the west, Brazil's borders lie in the foothills of the Andes. But the country does not extend to the high peaks and ranges of these mountains, so no parts of Brazil have cold mountain climates.

FLOODING AND DROUGHT

Many parts of Brazil experience regular, often heavy rainfall, so water is one of its main natural resources. The country's greatest reservoir is the Amazon basin, which contains rivers that discharge a quarter of the world's fresh running water into the Atlantic. Much of the basin is flooded in the wet season (January to June) due to high rainfall. Snowmelt in the Andes also adds to the water levels. Some land in the basin is permanently flooded. Other land is above flood level. Floating homes and houses built on stilts are precautions against flooding.

A contrasting part of Brazil is the semi-desert found inland from the Northeast coast. Known as the *sertão*, it has been plagued by droughts for centuries, destroying crops and causing a heavy loss of life. The lack of water is the result of irregular wind systems failing to bring rain. But poor land management has also created this dry scrubland. The difficult climate of this region has driven thousands of people to seek a new life in other parts of Brazil, especially the large cities.

CLIMATIC REGIONS

Brazil has four main climate zones, which relate closely to the country's land height and distance from the Equator. The graphs opposite (page 19) show each region's temperature and rainfall statistics in places that are representative of the region.

AMAZONIA

Amazonia is always hot and wet. Temperatures hardly vary, with midday averages of 26.9°C. Local conditions produce less rainfall in the winter months, but there is no dry season. Heat and humidity make conditions unpleasant for visitors who are not used to the wet tropics (see Manaus graph opposite).

A lightning storm marks the onset of the rainy season in the Brazilian Highlands.

TROPICAL EAST COAST

The east coast has a warm tropical climate. Between May and August, temperatures are cooled by the Trade Winds blowing in from the Atlantic and can drop to around 22°C. December to April are the wettest months, but conditions are less humid than in Amazonia (see Rio de Janeiro graph).

THE BRAZILIAN HIGHLANDS

Most of the Brazilian Highlands have distinct wet and dry seasons. These are exaggerated in the Northeast, where long periods of drought are common. The Northeast has similar temperatures to Amazonia, but the daily ranges are greater (see Remansão graph).

NON-TROPICAL SOUTH

The non-tropical South has rainfall throughout the year, although marked temperature differences occur between winter and summer. Cold Antarctic air can lead to frosts and occasional snowfalls inland. This cooler climate attracted migrants from central Europe, especially Germans (see Pôrto Alegre graph).

TEMPERATURE AND RAINFALL

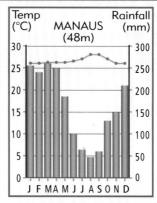

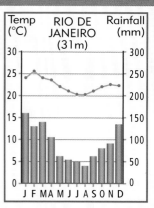

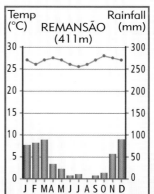

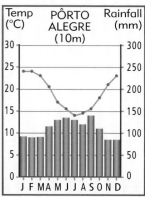

KEY:

Temp (°C)

Rainfall (mm)

Numbers in brackets show the city's height above sea level.

CLIMATE ZONES

Equator

Manaus

Remansão

N

| 0 | 500 | 1000km |
| 0 | | 600 miles |

Rio de Janeiro

Tropic of Capricorn

Pôrto Alegre

AMAZONIA: rainy tropical

BRAZILIAN HIGHLANDS: wet and dry tropical

EAST COAST: tropical

SOUTH: warm, rainy, non-tropical

Jaguars and other magnificent animals of Brazil's rain forests are threatened by poaching and destruction of their habitat.

Little can be grown on the *sertão* of the Northeast and grazing animals struggle to find enough food.

VEGETATION AND ECOSYSTEMS

The great variety of vegetation types and ecosystems in Brazil are the result of the country's topography and climate, together with soil and drainage differences. Its ecosystems are easily disturbed and the country has many examples of ecosystems that have been changed or are still being changed by human as well as physical processes.

TROPICAL RAIN FOREST

Brazil's hot, wet Amazonian climate supports tropical rain forest. This is a complex ecosystem consisting of broadleaf evergreen trees which shed old leaves and grow new ones simultaneously. The great variety of tree species (estimated at 2,500 in each square

kilometre) form a layered canopy. The trees at the top of the canopy reach heights of 60m. Beneath them are a collection of lower-growing species, linked with lianas (vines) and covered with mosses and other plants. The light beneath the canopy is so dim that few plants can grow on the forest floor.

Animals and insects play a major part in the rain-forest ecosystem. They help to produce the biomass (organic matter) and to recycle nutrients in the rain forest. There are a vast number of mammals, reptiles, birds and freshwater fish living in the rain forest, of many different species. Of the many thousands of insect species already catalogued, an even greater number are thought likely to remain undiscovered.

SCRUBLANDS

There are two large scrubland regions in Brazil. A large part of Mato Grosso state, in the Centre-West, is wild and largely undeveloped bush country. It is often regarded as Brazil's frontier 'wild west' country, where the dry and dusty landscape is home to poor farmers, Amerindians, miners, and rich ranchers with their hired hands (and often guns).

In the Northeast is the *sertão*, parched lands of brushwood and coarse grasses with large areas of *caatinga*, a vegetation of thick, impenetrable thorn shrubs and cacti. Brazil's scrublands are its most inhospitable environment.

THE ATLANTIC FORESTS

The thick forests that once covered the entire Atlantic coastal zone have been greatly reduced over the last 500 years, from an estimated 1.5 million km^2 in the sixteenth century to today's 10,000km^2. The forests have been cleared by agriculture, industry, lumbering and, above all, urbanisation. The coniferous forests of the south are greatly reduced, especially the areas of the distinctive araucaria or paraná pine tree.

GRASSLANDS

Grasslands are found in Brazil's highland and plateau areas, where there is a distinct dry season. Known as *cerrados*, these grassy upland plains with areas of woodland are similar to the African savannas. They have been greatly altered as a result of human interference, especially burning to clear land for farming. This has reduced the habitat for wildlife such as foxes, rheas and wolves. Other grasslands are found in the temperate areas of the South. They are linked with the pampas of Uruguay and Argentina.

The Pantanal wetlands are rich in freshwater fish and other wildlife.

Brazil has many 'protected' ecosystems, including over 350 national parks and wildlife reserves. One of the largest is the Pantanal, a huge swampy wetland with hundreds of species of freshwater fish, mammals, reptiles and birds. It is home to flesh-eating piranhas and the capybara, the world's largest rodent.

Tragically, the Pantanal's fragile ecosystem is under threat from river pollution caused by mining in Mato Grosso state and illegal hunting. On top of pollution, the region is the target of internationally organised poaching groups, which supply the world's fashion industry with the pelts and skins of jaguars and caymans. Although illegal, the skins fetch high prices on the black market. Reduced numbers of caymans means the piranha population growth is uncontrolled, which in turn affects other levels of fish and bird numbers. Despite government bans, large numbers of colourful birds from the Pantanal end up in pet shops throughout the world.

Itaipú Dam is part of the world's largest hydroelectric power station.

Although Brazil is rich in many natural resources, it is short of fossil fuels – coal, oil and natural gas. Coal is mined near Pôrto Alegre, but most of the country's coal supplies are imported from the USA, mainly in the form of coke (produced from coal). Charcoal (produced from wood) is used in many of Brazil's manufacturing industries, but its use is heavily scrutinised by environmentalists because of its effect on forest reduction.

POWER AND ENERGY

Oil has the highest demand because the country produces only one-fifth of its needs, and relies heavily on imports. These imports have been reduced by the discoveries of oil and natural gas supplies off the coast between Salvador and Vitória. Substantial reserves have allowed Brazil to develop some of the best offshore oil technology anywhere in the world.

HYDROELECTRICITY

Brazil has vast supplies of water, which makes it one of the world's largest potential sources of hydroelectric power (HEP). The steep valleys and escarpment edges in the highland and plateau areas may not be suitable for river transport, but they do provide good sites for the dams and reservoirs of hydroelectric power stations. Hydropower now generates over 90 per cent of Brazil's electricity.

CASE STUDY
THE ITAIPÚ DAM

In 2001, Itaipú Dam was the largest dam in the world. It is located on the Paraná river, close to Brazil's border with Paraguay. Fully operational in 1990, its 18 turbines are capable of producing 12.6 million kWh of energy, enough to supply the needs of southern Brazil and Paraguay. The dam was financed by foreign loans and is partly responsible for the country's huge national debts. It was one of the many giant projects of the military dictatorship, which ruled Brazil between 1964–1982. The amount of concrete used to build the dam would be enough to pave a two-lane highway across Europe, from Lisbon in Portugal to Moscow in Russia.

Many social and environmental issues result from Itaipú's 1,350km² reservoir. Over 40,000 families were forced off their land to make way for the reservoir, and the flooding involved a huge animal rescue programme. The vast new reservoir has created a microclimate that may cause future problems. Critics have long argued that smaller schemes nearer to the main economic centres would better serve Brazil's energy needs.

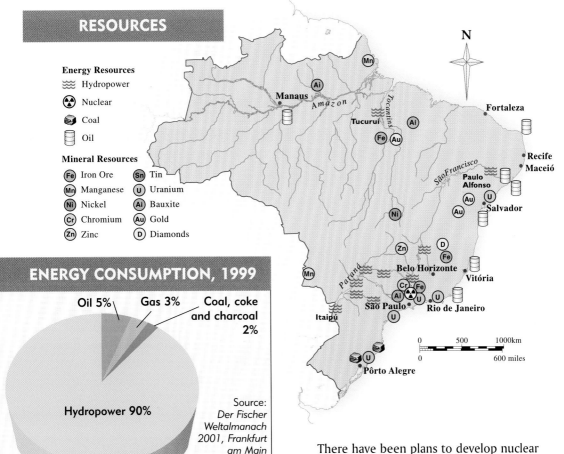

Energy Resources
- ≋ Hydropower
- ☢ Nuclear
- Coal
- Oil

Mineral Resources
- Fe Iron Ore
- Mn Manganese
- Ni Nickel
- Cr Chromium
- Zn Zinc
- Sn Tin
- U Uranium
- Ai Bauxite
- Au Gold
- D Diamonds

ENERGY CONSUMPTION, 1999

Oil 5% Gas 3% Coal, coke and charcoal 2%

Hydropower 90%

Source: *Der Fischer Weltalmanach 2001, Frankfurt am Main*

The Rio Paraná and its tributaries have hydroelectric power stations with reservoirs stretching for over 100km. The Rio São Francisco, which drains a large part of eastern Brazil, has large HEP stations near Belo Horizonte, and at Paulo Alfonso, inland from Maceió.

A pick-up truck stops to refuel with ethanol, a fuel made from sugar-cane alcohol.

There have been plans to develop nuclear power but only one plant, near São Paulo, has been built.

ETHANOL: ALTERNATIVE ENERGY

Brazil has made important contributions to the search for alternative renewable energy sources. In 1975 it launched its *Pre-alcool* programme, aimed at switching all motor vehicles from using petrol to ethanol (a type of alcohol) made from sugar cane.

By 1980, Brazilian production of petrol-only vehicles had been halted and replaced by engines burning either pure ethanol or gasohol, a mixture of petrol and ethanol. This led to a marked improvement in pollution levels in cities like São Paulo, and it made Brazil less dependent on oil imports.

In recent years, the *Pre-alcool* programme has suffered a series of setbacks linked to an increase in Brazil's own oil production, and conflicts between sugar-cane growers, distillers and the government over a fair price for ethanol.

MINERAL RESOURCES

Think of a mineral and Brazil probably mines it. The country's list of minerals is endless, from industrial ores and precious metals to gemstones, and huge areas of the country have not yet been surveyed. Brazil is a major world producer of iron ore, manganese, bauxite (for aluminium), nickel and tin. There are valuable deposits of uranium and thorium, and other minerals that are vital to today's hi-tech industries.

'GOLD-RUSH' CULTURE

Brazil's economic growth is closely associated with mineral discoveries. Prospecting is said to be in the Brazilian blood. When gold was found in the Brazilian Highlands in the 1690s, and diamonds in 1729, a great many people began searching. Fortune-hunters moved inland from the coast and were responsible for much of the country's early exploration and mapping. Many of the early mining settlements grew into rich colonial towns trading with São Paulo and Rio de Janeiro, from where precious minerals were shipped to Portugal. Between 1700 and 1800, nearly 1,000 tonnes of gold and 3 million carats of diamonds were exported from Brazil.

IRON ORE

The main concentration of early mining activity was in what became the state of Minas Gerais, its name meaning 'general mines'. This state still produces an incredible variety of minerals, but is particularly famous for its iron ore. South and south-west of Belo Horizonte, the state capital, there are rugged mountains.

Brazil's early fortune-hunters found gold. In gratitude, many churches were lavishly decorated with the metal.

Prospecting can begin at an early age. A good find can change people's lives.

The most prominent summit is the jagged Itabirito, which is partly natural but now mainly the result of mining. As much as 70 per cent of this peak is composed of iron ore. Around Belo Horizonte, the concentration of iron ore is reputed to be one of the world's highest. It is so great that in some of the city's suburbs, vehicles in neutral gear are drawn slowly uphill by magnetic force.

CASE STUDY
THE CARAJÁS PROJECT

The Carajás Project is situated in the Serra dos Carajás mountains in the state of Pará. This is where the world's largest-known iron-ore deposit is situated, which has Brazil's biggest concentration of minerals. Discovered in 1967, there is an estimated 18 billion tonnes of iron ore reserves in the region, which could supply the world for the next 500 years. Since the 1960s, massive opencast mining has transformed tropical rain forest into huge areas of dusty polluted landscape. Apart from iron ore, other minerals are mined and activities such as logging, charcoal production and aluminium smelting add more pollution to the landscape.

The project is focused on a hydropower dam at Tucuruí on the Tocantins river. The vision is to develop an industrial zone 400,000km^2 in area – equivalent to the size of California. To help iron ore exports, a new railway through the rain forest links the mining town of Carajás with the modernised port of São Luis on the Atlantic coast. Plans for cities, highways, steelworks and agribusinesses make this Brazil's largest and most expensive project, costing many billions of dollars. Many people think it is unlikely to succeed, which is one of the reasons why the Brazilian government has encouraged private investment in the area.

THE NEW GARIMPEIROS

Today Brazil produces a large proportion of the world's gemstones, including diamonds, topazes, amethysts and emeralds, but it is gold that continues to capture the imagination. It was again discovered in Pará state in the 1970s. This lead to a huge rush of *garimpeiros* (prospectors) from many parts of Brazil, but mainly from the poor Northeast. Opencast mines and shallow shafts are still dug by hand to form a massive lunar-like pit, where working conditions are grim and accidents frequent. Estimates vary as to the number of fortune-seekers but in the dry season, 60,000–100,000 might be involved.

Massive opencast mining has transformed vast areas of the Brazilian landscape, much of which was once forest land.

Amazonia is a vast area of water and forest, a fragile ecosystem that is easily disrupted.

The Amazon rain forest, of which 60 per cent belongs to Brazil, is a vast, complex and fragile ecosystem. It is home to one-tenth of the earth's entire plant and animal species and holds one-fifth of the earth's freshwater resources. It is like a massive 'green lung' through which the earth breathes, which means that any interference has an impact on the rest of the world. The full effects of rain-forest destruction are not yet properly understood.

THE MIGHTY RIVER

From its source in the Peruvian Andes to its mouth at the Atlantic, the Amazon river flows over a distance of 6,440km, most of which is through the world's largest rain forest. The Amazon rain forest has an area of about 6.5 million km². Numerous huge tributaries add to the river's volume. Both the tributaries and the main river provide access to all the main settlements in Amazonia and have made those settlements possible as trading centres. The city of Manaus lies 1,600km inland, close to where the Negro tributary joins the main river. The city is a collection and distribution centre for the towns and villages along the river and is served by ocean-going liners.

The Amazon river discharges 4.5 trillion gallons of water a day into the Atlantic, an amount capable of supplying every US household for six months. The river system also carries immense amounts of sediment from its source to the sea, but the flow is too strong for a true delta to form. Instead, the Amazon reaches the sea in a complicated system of channels and islands. The largest of these islands, Marajó, is the size of Switzerland. At the river's mouth, the north and south banks are further apart than the distance between London and Paris.

THE RUBBER TRADE

Compared to the rest of Brazil, Amazonia was economically poor until commercial tapping of the rubber tree began in the nineteenth century. The Amerindians had been harvesting the latex from the rubber tree for hundreds of years,

The large city of Belém, at the mouth of the Amazon, is the region's main port. Both Belém and Manaus, a city in the heart of Amazonia, grew rich on the products of the forest.

making shoes and waterproof containers. They called the tree *cahuchu*, meaning 'weeping tree', from the drops of latex that oozed from the bark. As manufacturers in the USA and Europe discovered how to make products from the rubber such as raincoats, hoses and shoes, the rubber industry grew. At first all the rubber came from the wild. Harvesting was difficult because the rubber tree grows on its own and often far apart in the rain forest.

In the early twentieth century, the invention of the automobile and rubber tyres created a high demand for rubber, which led to a rapid growth in Amazonia's population as people moved in to make their fortune. By 1910, Brazil was supplying 88 per cent of the world's rubber, controlled from Belém and Manaus by rich rubber barons. But the boom was short-lived. By 1911 Brazil was unable to compete with the huge rubber plantations of Malaya, developed from seeds smuggled out of Amazonia.

Attempts to establish rubber plantations in Amazonia, such as the Henry Ford project in the Tapajós Valley, have ended in failure. This project, which started in 1928, involved extensive forest clearance and the rubber trees eventually died from disease brought on by soil exhaustion – a lesson still to be learned in Amazonia. The project was sold to the Brazilian government in 1945. There are still rubber tappers in the forest and special reserves protect the trees. Output, however, is a pale reflection of rubber's boom years.

Rubber tappers still work in the rain forest, but they may tap from trees in extractive reserves, such as this one in the state of Acré.

DEVELOPMENT IN AMAZONIA

Over the last 100 years, numerous attempts have been made to open up the Amazon's frontiers to make the most of what was seen as a valuable resource going to waste. The government cooperated with foreign companies on a variety of projects. There were three main objectives to these projects:

1. To populate some of Brazil's northern and western frontiers in order to strengthen its control over disputed territories.
2. To encourage landless peasant farmers into the region.
3. To search for and exploit minerals and other resources.

CASE STUDY
THE TRANS-AMAZONIA HIGHWAY

The Trans-Amazonia Highway (see map on page 11), was begun in the 1960s. It crosses southern Amazonia from the Atlantic (via the Belém-Brasília highway) to the Peruvian border, a distance of 5,400km. It is another of Brazil's grand and expensive schemes, part of the plan to open up Amazonia and attract people from the dry Northeast region. The highway construction has been much criticised for causing extensive forest destruction and the eviction of Amerindians. Only a small section is asphalted, and both weather erosion and under-use has meant it is deteriorating rapidly.

The construction of the Trans-Amazonia Highway destroyed large areas of forest.

ROAD BUILDING

After the 1950s, a large programme of road building took place in Brazil. In Amazonia the aim was to encourage people to settle and develop the region. But road building through the Amazon, such as the Trans-Amazonia Highway, has destroyed huge swathes of forest, sometimes for little purpose. Many roads are unfinished or poorly maintained and have been reduced to pot-holes and quagmires.

LAND CLEARANCE

Clearing land for cultivation has also been a failure. The rain forest appears to be supported by fertile soils, but this is not true. The soil relies on the remains of plants and animals for nutrition, so when vegetation is cleared for farming, the soils become thin and infertile within two to three years and few crops can be grown. The Amerindians understand this important relationship and have special ways of farming the land (see page 30). But the migrants who move to Amazonia from places like the Northeast do not. A few years after moving to the region and clearing a plot of land, many find that they can grow little food. The migrants often find that they have moved from one rural poverty trap to another.

CATTLE RANCHES

Both migrant farmers and Amerindians have had to compete with large companies who ruthlessly displace people and use their land for vast cattle ranches. Ecologists agree that the conversion of rain forest to grazing land for animals is the worst possible use of the land. Toxic weeds are a problem to animals and the only way to get rid of the weeds is by burning, which causes air pollution and disturbs the ecosystem. Most ranches are abandoned after five years, leaving a totally degraded landscape.

DAM BUILDING

The building of dams and the creation of huge reservoirs for hydroelectric power stations have damaged Amazonia's ecology. As forest

Hundreds of thousands of landless peasant families like these have moved into Amazonia from other parts of Brazil, looking for a better life.

vegetation is flooded, it decomposes, rots, and is continuously washed into the reservoirs, emitting large amounts of carbon dioxide and methane. These are two important greenhouse gases. Calculations show that the Turcuruí reservoir, part of the Carajás project in Pará state, has had 60 per cent more impact on global warming than a coal-fired power station generating the same amount of energy.

Other damage from dam building is caused by the workers themselves. Dam construction requires huge amounts of labour. Migrant labourers come from all parts of Brazil. They are housed in temporary accommodation, with bars and brothels. Such concentrations of people can lead to health hazards including the spread of tuberculosis, AIDS and sexually transmitted diseases.

Many of the large-scale projects to develop Amazonia have been expensive failures, and most have resulted in the disruption of the rain-forest ecosystem and the loss of Amerindian homelands.

In the state of Acre, large expanses of forest have been cleared for cattle pasture. Only the valuable brazil nut trees have been spared.

AMERINDIANS

The Amerindian groups have been the main victims of rain-forest destruction, which has increasingly destroyed their land and their livelihood. These are the people who really understand the forest, live in harmony with the ecosystem and could teach the rest of the world how to protect the environment.

SUBSISTENCE ECONOMIES

The Amerindians use the forest's resources in two ways: basic hunting and gathering, and the more advanced farming. This is a type of subsistence economy, where they only take from the rain forest what they need themselves. Hunting and gathering is based on the great variety of food available in the rain forest – animal, plant and insect life. This lifestyle is a wandering or nomadic existence in which men hunt and women gather foods from the forest.

Amerindian farming is also known as 'shifting cultivation'. After clearing a patch of forest by cutting and burning away the vegetation (leaving food-providing trees such as the banana and kola nut), the ashes are dug into the soil as a fertiliser. A variety of crops are grown, such as yams and manioc, as well as beans, pumpkins and tobacco. Without the vegetation cover and forest nutrients, the soil loses its fertility after two or three years, so

A small forest clearing is the first stage in subsistence cultivation.

the farmers move on to clear a new plot. The land they have abandoned is left fallow for about 10 years to allow the growth of secondary forest. Many rain-forest dwellers prefer to work these areas rather than primary forest, because they are easier to clear. This relieves pressure on the primary forest and minimises its destruction.

Shifting cultivation allows the forest to recover after its soil has been used for growing crops. In contrast, recent peasant migrants to Amazonia have used 'slash-and-burn' techniques to clear the land, where the soil is not allowed to recover its fertility and suffers from erosion. These migrants practise what is known as a 'robber economy' – the over-exploitation of renewable resources.

PROTECTING THE AMERINDIANS

The Brazilian Amerindians are protected by FUNAI, the government Amerindians Agency. Some 850,000km^2 (10 per cent of Brazil's territory) has been set aside as reservation land where, technically, they are free to practise their traditional lifestyles. However, the Amerindians continue to suffer from ruthless land encroachment and dispossession

CASE STUDY
FOREST MEDICINE

Living as part of the forest ecosystem, the Amerindians have a detailed knowledge of the various properties and uses of plants. Scientific investigation has shown that many hundreds of species have important medicinal uses. In fact, one-in-four of the ingredients found in a Western chemist's shop come from the leaves, roots, fruits and barks of forest plants. Tribal shamans, whose knowledge is handed down orally, know of forest plants that can help cure a great variety of medical conditions. If the forest and the Amerindians are wiped out, this knowledge will disappear.

Medicinal plants and extracts from the forest can be found for sale in most Brazilian markets.

by brute force. The now-famous Yanomami, an Amerindian group discovered in Roraima in 1973, were people with traditional ways forced to confront the modern age. The transition was not easy. Today their numbers have been greatly reduced by the influx of lumber companies and mineral speculators.

Amerindians use the forest resources carefully. This man has collected vines for basket-making in the rain forest near Manaus.

FAIR TRADE

There are some examples of fair dealing with the Amerindians, however. The Kayapo harvest brazil nuts for the British company The Body Shop. Oil from the nuts is used in cosmetics and the Amerindians are paid a suitable wage for their work. In Germany, Spain and Portugal, other 'green-conscious' companies have fair trading relationships with the Amerindians. Their products are found in many department stores and chemists.

Harvesting the coffee cherry depends on labour-intensive hand-picking methods.

Brazil is one of the world's most important farming countries. Agriculture employs a quarter of the working population and provides 40 per cent of exports. The most important product is coffee. Brazil is the world's leading producer and exporter of coffee. On the world market, the coffee industry is second only to the oil industry in importance and value, with over 25 million people around the world gaining their living from its production and sale.

CASE STUDY
COFFEE

Coffee plantations occupy some 2.4 million hectares of Brazil. São Paulo, Minas Gerais and Paraná are the major coffee-producing states, where a combination of suitable landscape, climate and rich soil provide ideal conditions for the crop.

The coffee bean is the seed of the coffee tree. It grows inside a fruit, called a 'cherry', and develops over a period of six to nine months. The trees are planted in rows on well-drained hillsides, mostly at altitudes of between 300 and 1,000m. The cherries need maximum sunshine to ripen and are sensitive to high wind, drought and sudden falls in temperature. Heavy frosts ruined large harvests in 1994 and output was reduced in 2001 by prolonged water shortage. Both years resulted in sharp rises in coffee prices. The price of coffee is controlled by the Brazilian Coffee Institute by regulating the amount of coffee grown and sold on the world market each year. Coffee has important economic and political value in world trade transactions.

Coffee estates are labour intensive, especially at harvest time. Cherries on the same bush ripen at different times, which means that harvesting has to be done by hand and each bush requires several visits by pickers. Once collected, other tasks include separating the bean from its outer pulp before drying and roasting. There are a number of roasting procedures to determine the coffee's flavour, aroma and strength. These processes, together with storage, packaging and shipment, explain the high market cost of coffee.

Brazil's other major export crops are sugar, cocoa, soybeans and maize. Thanks to its climate, almost every kind of fruit is grown, from tropical to temperate varieties. The enormous output of citrus fruit is exported mainly as concentrated juice. A variety of nuts and spices also find their way to the shelves of the world's supermarkets.

CASH CROPS AND PLANTATIONS

From the early days of colonialism, Brazilian agriculture has been based on the production of one cash crop for export. Beginning with sugar cane, other crops were cotton, cocoa,

Many landless families travel in search of farm work, such as the tending and harvesting of field crops.

rubber and coffee. These crops were, and in some states still are, grown on plantations. Before the twentieth century, the plantations used slave labour on large estates, called *fazendas*. Today, the same estates employ casual workers on short-term contracts. Many people, known as *caboclos*, travel the Brazilian countryside in search of seasonal jobs, moving from one plantation after another as they follow the work available.

MIGRANT WORKERS

For many rural workers, this seasonal migration is a necessity. Brazil is a country of extreme agricultural inequality, with many thousands of landless families struggling to make a living. According to the World Bank, 43 per cent of the country's farmed land belongs to only 0.3 per cent of landowners, many of which are now multinational companies. Government land reform and redistribution movements have had little effect in changing land ownership since its main action has been to provide land in Amazonia, where farming methods have not been successful.

ECONOMIC STRUCTURE, 1997 (% GDP CONTRIBUTION)

Agriculture 14%
Services 50%
Industry 36%

Source: CIA World Factbook, 2000

AGRICULTURE

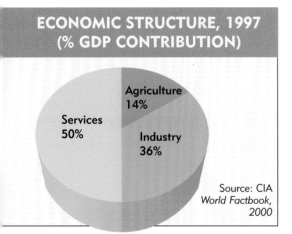

Manaus
Recife
Salvador
Belo Horizonte
São Paulo
Rio de Janeiro
Pôrto Alegre

N

0   500   1000km
0   600 miles

Plantation farming: cocoa, cotton, tobacco and sugar

Plantations and arable: coffee, sugar cane and cereals

Extensive and intensive farming: cattle, sheep, soya, grains, fruits and vegetables

Tropical forest: subsistence farming and ranching

Extensive farming: cattle and pigs

Rubber

Despite some mechanisation, sugar cane is a labour-intensive crop that uses farming methods little different to those of colonial times.

THE NORTHEAST: SUGAR, COCOA AND COLONIALISM

The Northeast is Brazil's problem region, characterised by poverty, underemployment, and loss of people through migration. One of the main reasons why the region is unable to support its population is related to the unequal distribution of land. The region is divided between a relatively small number of extremely rich landowners and masses of poor, illiterate farmworkers, most of whom have no land at all. This situation is the survival of a system that dates from colonial times.

THE COLONIAL SYSTEM

The Northeast was the first part of Brazil to be settled by Europeans. They introduced the plantation system and the early landowners grew rich on crops grown for export, first sugar cane in the sixteenth century and later cocoa in the 1850s. The sugar empires depended entirely on African slave labour, while cocoa relied on grossly underpaid and landless farm labourers. Technically these labourers were 'economic slaves', like the majority of rural workers in the Northeast today. 'Without land you are nothing' is a Northeast saying.

PLANTATIONS AND POVERTY

The ownership of massive estates by a powerful minority is responsible for the Northeast's continuing poverty. The *fazendeiros* (estate owners) have become Brazil's ruling class once again. They have a strong influence on the governments of the Northeast states and, as a result, with the federal government in Brasília. Many estate owners are unprepared to part with their land or agree to agrarian reform. Instead they support a system that pays very low wages for long hours and often dangerous working conditions, and one that hires and sacks workforces at will.

SUGAR AND COCOA

The Northeast's coastal areas, with their tropical temperatures and high rainfall levels, are well suited to growing sugar cane and cocoa, which employs most of the region's rural workers. Both crops require minimal levels of technology but a large supply of unskilled labour. Plantations have replaced much of the original coastal rain forest, which now only exists in tiny pockets. However, the plantations' soil has been impoverished as a result of monoculture, where the cultivation of the same crop on the same piece of land quickly uses up nutrients.

Brazil is the world's largest producer of sugar, accounting for 13 per cent of the global total. The refined product is exported throughout the world with Russia, Nigeria and Middle Eastern countries being the largest markets. The country's own demand for sugar has also increased. This is linked to the growth in soft drink and confectionery products, as well as the production of ethanol (see page 23). Outside the Northeast, sugar cane is also important in parts of the South and Southeast.

Although still an important crop in the Northeast, the world demand for chocolate made from cocoa beans has fallen. This has resulted in lower prices for cocoa, which have forced landowners to reduce their output and cut the number of rural jobs. The main chocolate-consuming countries are the USA and those of Western Europe, such as Germany, Belgium, the Netherlands and the UK. The trade is controlled by multinational companies (see page 39) and Nestlé has many processing plants in Brazil. Cheaper substitutes for cocoa, including chopped cabbage and pig's blood, are now used in 'chocolate' products instead of cocoa beans. On top of reduced world demand for the beans, Brazil's cocoa zone is plagued by a fungus disease called 'Witches Broom', which frequently destroys entire plantations.

THE BACKLANDS

Inland from the coast is the *sertão*, which covers a large area of the Northeast. This barren region has become arid and infertile as a result of drought and land mismanagement, including over-grazing. Many thousands of people have died over the years due to starvation and disease. Better-quality lands, such as those found in some of the river valleys, have been claimed by powerful cattle barons. The rest of the population has been

The Northeast's tropical climate is ideal for growing citrus fruits.

pushed into less favourable areas and drought regularly forces them to seek refuge in the coastal cities. They are known as the *flagelados*, the 'scourged ones', and are Brazil's most socially destitute and desperate victims of poverty.

Despite its social and economic problems, fish is one foodstuff the Northeast has in abundance.

THE SOUTH: RANCHES AND VINEYARDS

No part of Brazil is more different to the Northeast than the country's South region. Since most of the South lies below the Tropic of Capricorn it has four better-marked seasons, with frosts and occasional snowfalls in winter. This climate helped to attract large numbers of immigrants from Italy, Germany, Poland and Russia. They give the region a distinctive European character, especially in the country towns and villages, which have kept many of their European customs, traditions and, in places, dialects merged with Portuguese (see case study below).

INTENSIVE AND EXTENSIVE FARMING

Two distinctive farming economies exist in the South, influenced by physical conditions. Along the coast, particularly in the state of Santa Catarina, intensive farming is practised on family-run farms. The farms produce a variety of grains, fruits (including vines) and vegetables, and raise cattle, sheep, pigs and

poultry. This mixed farming system greatly differs from the monoculture of Brazil's plantation system. Based on European customs, farming cycles, particularly harvests, are celebrated with colourful festivals.

CASE STUDY
EUROPEAN CULTURE: VINEYARDS AND BREWERIES

Inside a cellar of a major winery in Rio Grande do Sul.

Italian immigrants first introduced vines to the valleys and coastal hillsides of Rio Grande do Sul at the end of the nineteenth century. Today this is where 90 per cent of Brazilian wine is produced. The villages and small farms of the area, with their cheeses, salamis, pastas and wine cellars, retain the air of Italy about them. The introduction of Californian and other grape varieties from Europe has improved the quality of Brazil's wines, which are finding new markets throughout the world.

German immigrants also brought beer-making skills to the South and were responsible for the region's breweries. The annual *Oktoberfest*, a beer festival modelled on the original festival in Munich, is held in the town of Blumenau every year and is now the second-largest festival in Brazil, after the Rio Carnival. Visits by German orchestras, folk-dancing displays and German food make sure German culture is preserved in the region.

The South's temperate grasslands are ideal for grazing cattle.

In the South, the proud *gauchos* retain their culture and traditions.

In contrast, the rolling inland grasslands of the South are areas of extensive crop and animal farming. Together with parts of São Paulo state they form what is called Brazil's 'breadbasket', growing wheat, maize, rice and soybeans. They also have the country's largest cattle ranches and sheep populations. These temperate grasslands are some of the leading areas of commercial grazing in the world. The climate and rich grasses allow year-round grazing, and the animals are also fed on grains and other fodder crops.

Brazil is the world's fourth-largest beef producer, with the South having a quarter of the country's estimated 150 million head of cattle. However, the region is losing this position to the Southeast and Centre-West, where interbreeding with zebus (a species of humped oxen) and Angolan stock has produced cattle that are better at surviving the drier conditions of the Brazilian Highlands. A growing number of the South's former ranches are now dominated by endless expanses of soybean crops which, ironically, are exported to feed European cattle.

The South American cowboy, the *gaucho*, is a very common sight in Brazil's South, as in other cattle farming areas in Brazil. *Gauchos* roam the grasslands with large numbers of cattle or sheep, helping to provide Brazil with meat, leather and wool for its textile industries. One of the main centres of *gaucho* traditions is Santana do Livramento, on the border with Uruguay. Here a unique culture has developed, a mixture of Portuguese and Spanish, together with Italian and German lifestyles.

Ranching is so important to Brazil that it has developed its own distinctive festivals, many of which originated in the *sertão* lands of the Northeast. Rodeos are common gatherings in the cattle towns, with one of the most important held at Uruguaiana, on the Argentina border. The riding and other skilled events of the rodeo attract competitors from all over Brazil, Uruguay and Argentina. Like North American cowboys, some are professionals, earning a living by moving from one event to another.

INDUSTRY, DEVELOPMENT AND TRANSPORT

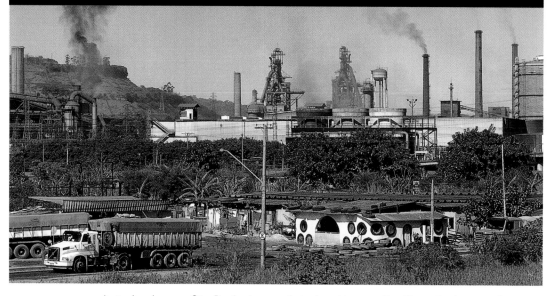

A steelworks near São Paulo. Iron and steel-making are Brazil's major heavy industries.

Brazil is a newly industrialising country (NIC) with a wealthier economy than any other South American country. An important characteristic of an NIC is the growth of its manufacturing industry and products for export. From an essentially agricultural economy up until the mid-twentieth century, Brazil now has an economy where industry is of increasing importance. Manufactured goods today account for more than two-thirds of total exports.

DEVELOPMENT POLICIES

The change from agriculture to manufacturing in Brazil's economy is the result of deliberate government policy. The policy supports two strategies: the first is the development of its export market, where products are sold abroad. The second is the development of manufacturing for the country's own market, especially the production of consumer goods. The government restricts certain goods from abroad to be imported, which has greatly benefited Brazil's domestic industries.

INDUSTRIALISATION IN THE SOUTHEAST

Brazil's steel and other mineral-based industries, transport equipment, petrochemicals, machinery and food products

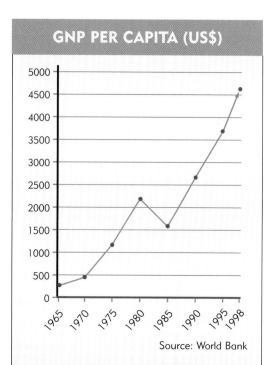

GNP PER CAPITA (US$)

Source: World Bank

Most heavy industrial products are exported through the port of Santos, the closest port to São Paulo.

Although it began as just a few assembly plants in the early twentieth century, the industry currently produces an average of one million vehicles a year. They are built using components made in Brazil rather than being imported. The country ranks tenth place among the world's motor vehicle producers, and General Motors, Ford, Fiat, Toyota, Volkswagen and Mercedes-Benz all have production and assembly plants in the country. In addition to cars and trucks, there is an important output of tractors and other agricultural vehicles, motor cycles and railway parts.

AIRCRAFT AND SPACE RESEARCH

Brazilians were among the pioneers of early aviation, but their aircraft industry only really began 25 years ago. It has rapidly grown to become the sixth-largest in the world. The main company, Embraer, exports commercial and military aircraft throughout the world. The company is also leading the move towards pure jet travel on the country's air routes.

Brazil's aerospace industry has also seen rapid growth, which has led to remote surveillance and satellite monitoring of the country's huge territory. This plays an important role in environmental protection, especially in Amazonia and other sparsely populated areas.

have played major roles in its economic expansion. The country's most industrialised region is the Southeast, especially the 'industrial triangle' formed by the huge conurbations of São Paulo, Rio de Janeiro and Belo Horizonte. São Paulo state has about 50 per cent of Brazilian industry and the city is South America's largest industrial centre.

THE MULTINATIONALS

São Paulo is the headquarters for most of the foreign multinational companies that control a large part of Brazilian industry. Their growth is due to the government policy of reducing state control of industry and increasing privatisation and foreign investment. Multinational companies have been able to profit from Brazil's huge foreign debt (see page 54) and its repayments to global institutions. In 1999, 14 of Brazil's 20 largest companies in terms of sales revenue were owned by foreign companies. They include oil consortiums such as Shell, Texaco and Esso; Carrefour (supermarkets); Nestlé (food products); Gessy Lever (hygiene products) and most of the world's automobile companies.

THE AUTOMOBILE INDUSTRY

The automobile industry is Brazil's top manufacturing sector in terms of sales figures.

Workers at the Embraer aircraft factory put the finishing touches to a new passenger jet.

TYPES OF TRANSPORT BY JOURNEY, 2000

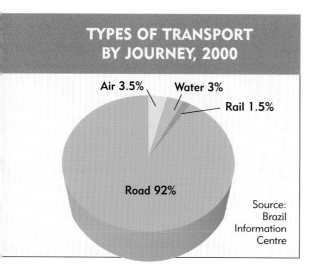

Air 3.5% Water 3%

Rail 1.5%

Road 92%

Source: Brazil Information Centre

Modern metro systems, like this one in São Paulo, try to ease traffic congestion in the city by encouraging people to take public transport instead of the car.

Bus journeys in Brazil can be lengthy, often needing overnight stops. This is where the *rodoviaria*, or bus terminal plays an important role. Usually located on the outskirts of a city, it is much more than a busy bus station. As well as dealing with timetables and tickets, it is also a retail, services and leisure centre, catering to the needs of travellers whose journeys can last a number of days and nights. Brazilian bus services are mostly efficient and of high quality. They belong to hundreds of private companies and connect all inhabited parts of the country, even where road surfaces are little more than rural tracks. However Brazil is a developing country, illustrated by the poor quality of transport in its most isolated areas.

A bustling bus station in Brasília.

TRANSPORT

Brazil's vast size and endless stretches of rain forest, *sertão* and *cerrado* make many land journeys long and difficult. For those who can afford it, air travel is the most efficient means of travel, but most Brazilians rely on the bus or, in Amazonia, the river boats.

ROADS

A large amount of money is spent on Brazilian roads, which transport over 90 per cent of the country's population and goods. There are over 1.6 million km of roads, but only some 7 per cent are asphalted, making driving conditions difficult in wet weather. The densest network (see map page 11) is in the Southeast region, where modern motorways link São Paulo, Rio de Janeiro, Belo Horizonte and Brasília. The busiest stretch of highway is that linking São Paulo with the port of Santos.

Practically all the state capitals are linked by paved roads and many have modern expressways. But traffic is a huge problem in and around the large conurbations, where routes are constantly clogged with cars, lorries and buses. Exhaust fumes pollute the air and São Paulo, with its added industrial toxins, is one of the world's most polluted cities.

RAILWAYS

The main railway network is also in the Southeast (see map page 11), but in proportion to the roads it is relatively small. Most of the railway lines were built in the nineteenth century to carry minerals and agricultural produce to the ports for export. There is still an extensive freight network, but passenger services are limited, slow and more expensive than buses. The busiest route is the luxury night service between São Paulo and Rio de Janeiro. Some lines are specifically aimed at tourists. They use steam-powered trains on routes through scenic mountains and colonial countrysides.

AIR TRAVEL

Brazil has one of the largest internal air networks in the world, with the busiest route, São Paulo-to-Rio de Janeiro, operating a daily shuttle service. As well as the major city airports, every state capital has an airport or airfield where air taxis, or 'teco-teco' flights, are popular with business people. As in other countries with large, remote areas, air services are often social and medical lifelines.

TIME TO BRASÍLIA (HOURS)

CITY	BY AIR	BY BUS
Belo Horizonte	1.00	12
São Paulo	1.25	16
Rio de Janeiro	1.25	20
Pôrto Alegre	2.20	33
Manaus	2.30	35
Foz do Iguaçu	3.25	28

Source: Brazil Information Centre

RIVER BOATS

Tourists can see the Amazon from the deck of a cruise ship, but most Brazilians are dependent on the slow and uncomfortable steamers that travel between the various ferry-boat terminals. A two-hour air journey between Belém and Manaus increases to between four and five days by river. Travelling by river boat is monotonous, tough-going and lacking all but the most basic facilities. A hammock on deck is more comfortable than a crowded and poorly ventilated cabin.

The Amazon river ports are always scenes of colourful activity.

Olinda (in the foreground) and Recife (behind) show both historical and modern development. Olinda grew wealthy from sugar in colonial times.

Brazil has a great variety of towns and cities, ranging from 'pioneer' towns in Amazonia and Mato Grosso state to massive conurbations. The variety of settlements is partly due to the physical size and diversity of the country, but it is also due to Brazil's history and the origins of its immigrants.

COLONIAL TOWNS

Brazil's earliest towns grew from trading posts along the Atlantic, and the inland centres of prospecting, which depended on the coast for export links with Europe. The construction of forts at places like Recife, Salvador and Rio de Janeiro provided centres for urban growth.

The plan and architecture of these colonial towns were greatly influenced by the Portuguese settlers and many of these centres, particularly in the Northeast and Minas Gerais, are now protected heritage sites. However, they are surrounded by largely unplanned modern urban sprawl.

URBANISATION

From the middle of the nineteenth century, many of Brazil's historic towns were altered by a rapid process of urbanisation. The main cause of this growth was immigration. Urbanisation continues to the present day with 81 per cent of the country's population classified as living in towns and cities (see graph on page 43). The annual urban growth rate is 3 per cent, which means that many Brazilian cities will double their population in a few decades.

Population figures are difficult to calculate because there are many thousands, especially

BRAZIL'S LARGEST CITIES, 1999	
	Population (millions)
São Paulo	16.6
Rio de Janeiro	10.3
Belo Horizonte	4.6
Salvador	3.1
Fortaleza	2.3

Source: *Der Fischer Weltalmanach 2001, Frankfurt am Main*

Poor migrants with large families swell the numbers in Brazil's big cities.

Traffic congestion in São Paulo is just one of the problems caused by rural-urban migration.

those living in *favela* districts, who are not on urban registers. This means that population totals could possibly be doubled.

RURAL-URBAN MIGRATION

The movement of people from the countryside to the cities is a major cause of urbanisation. Most migrants head for the Southeast, which dominates Brazil's economy. The 'pull factors', or attractions, are promises of better economic and social lifestyles. Most migrants come from the Northeast, where the 'push factor' is poverty. Rural migrants have large families, bringing even more people to the cities.

Urban growth brings other problems. Housing, transport and services cannot cope with the sheer volume of newcomers, traffic jams cause chaos and air pollution is often life-threatening. Many wealthier people are moving out of Brazil's large cities to set up homes and business in smaller towns, which offer a better quality of life.

CASE STUDY
BAHIA – THE 'PUSH FACTORS'

Poverty and a low quality of life force people to leave the Northeast. In Bahia state, only 18 out of 415 cities have basic sanitation and out of every 1,000 infants, 43 do not survive their first year. About 40 per cent of Bahia's schools are closed due to lack of funds and half the state's population is illiterate. The number of unemployed is 30 per cent of the workforce. The government has been unable to curb the drift to the Southeast of those in search of a living wage.

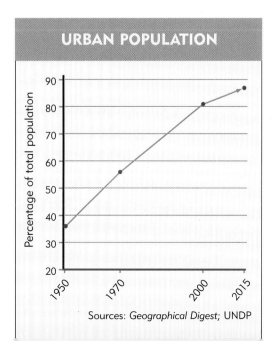

URBAN POPULATION

Sources: *Geographical Digest*; UNDP

RIO DE JANEIRO AND SÃO PAULO – THE 'URBAN GIANTS'

RIO DE JANEIRO ('RIO')

In January 1502, Portuguese explorers visited Guanabara Bay. Mistaking it for a river, they called it Rio de Janeiro, 'River of January'. Had they sailed further into the bay they would have discovered that it forms a huge natural harbour, one of the largest, safest and most beautiful in the world. The city of Rio spreads around the irregular shores of this great harbour, which is a complex of rocky peninsulas, sheltered havens, extensive beaches, dome-shaped mountains and palm-fringed islands. The shape of the harbour makes Rio one of the world's most dramatically sited cities, but also one of the most difficult in terms of urban planning.

Rio began its history as a fortified Portuguese outpost, but grew to prominence as the export port for the mineral wealth and agricultural produce of the inland areas. In 1763, the city replaced Salvador as Brazil's capital and for a short time in the nineteenth century it became capital of the entire Portuguese Empire, including Portugal itself. Many buildings survive from the city's colonial days.

ABOVE: Busy beaches and boulevards are some of the characteristics of Rio de Janeiro.

BELOW: Architectural giants cramp older buildings in São Paulo, Brazil's economic powerhouse.

Today Rio is famous for its intense and varied cultural life. It is said that the city's main industry is the pursuit of pleasure, but this ignores its role as a major manufacturing, services and financial centre. The city lost its capital status to Brasília in 1960 but it has not lost its urban attractions. There are wealthy districts of luxury apartment blocks, and expensive shopping boulevards on a par with those in European and North American cities. The image of 'bright lights' is a magnet to many Brazilian migrants, thousands of whom find themselves living in one of the many *favelas* that crowd the swampy coastal areas and steep mountain sides. Towering over the city, on the 709m-high Corcovado mountain, is a huge statue of Christ. There is argument as to whether he guards an urban 'Garden of Eden' or a 'concrete jungle'.

SÃO PAULO

The people of São Paulo often comment that whereas Rio's *Cariocas* are fond of enjoying themselves they, the *Paulistas*, are dedicated to enterprise and hard work. There is certainly a different atmosphere in what is Brazil's largest city and economic powerhouse. Over 20,000 industrial plants of all types and sizes employing 600,000 workers are concentrated in the city and its surrounding towns. São Paulo is also the major financial centre of Brazil, with nearly 2,000 banking agencies.

The city's rapid growth and high-rise development has obliterated almost everything of old São Paulo, which was founded by Portuguese Jesuit priests in 1554. They chose a plateau site for their mission at 760m above sea level, but only 72km from the coast. Here a number of river valleys fanned into the interior. *Bandeirantes*, adventurers and fortune-hunters who explored the Brazilian hinterland in the fifteenth and sixteenth centuries, also used the site as a base. Some of the modern expressways radiating from São Paulo follow routes opened up by the *bandeirantes* and *tropeiros* (cattle drovers).

The old colonial settlement was transformed by the coffee boom of the late nineteenth century, which brought massive immigration. São Paulo became a migrant city, which it continues to be today. The port of Santos grew with São Paulo to become the world's largest coffee-exporting port. It now serves the industries of the Southeast with some of the most modern dockside installations in South America.

From the older central districts, São Paulo spreads in all directions like an endless urban jungle of high-rise concrete, steel and glass buildings, carved through by motorways, boulevards, viaducts and railway tracks. Close to the city centre are the wealthy villas of the rich, enclosed by lush gardens. These are the homes of those who made São Paulo rich. A visit to a *favela* shows a very different side of life in the city.

The lush watered gardens of São Paulo's wealthy are a sharp contrast to the city's *favelas*.

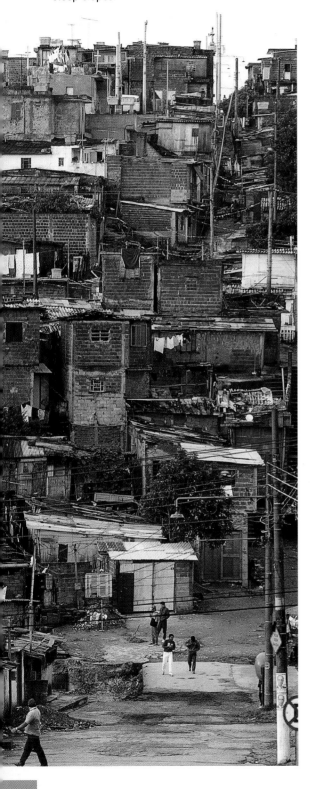

Rio has some of Brazil's oldest and largest *favelas*, many clinging precariously to the city's steep slopes.

URBAN DEPRIVATION

Brazil's urban growth has created many problems. One of the major ones is to match people with jobs. Many migrants, once they move to the city, find it virtually impossible to find a job and few other hopes are met. Their home turns out to be at best an inner-city slum, at worst a squatter's shack.

THE FAVELAS

Unable to find jobs and afford rented accommodation, Brazil's urban poor have built shanty towns on land to which they have no legal right. In Rio this usually means the hillsides that surround the city. The shanty towns take the name *favelas* from the flower that grows wild on these slopes, but there is nothing floral about the *favelas*. It is said that the only advantage enjoyed by the *favelados*, or slum dwellers, are the best views over Guanabara Bay. Seen from the shore, the *favelas* form a bizarre backdrop to the tourist resorts of Copacabana and Ipanema.

Rio is not the only city with *favelas*, but it has nearly 500, some of them the oldest and the largest with populations estimated as high as 200,000. Most of the homes are little more than shacks built from any available material – wood, corrugated iron, plastic sheets, cardboard and reeds. Inside are one or two rooms with no running water, sanitation or electricity, unless it is illegally tapped. Typhoid, dysentery and other diseases are common in these overcrowded environments, where rubbish rots in unpaved alleyways.

The *favelados* are engaged in a daily struggle for survival made worse by a hazardous physical environment. Heavy rains on these steep slopes, weakened by construction work and the sheer weight of people, mean that flimsy structures can be carried downslope. There are frequent heavy death tolls as a result of these landslides.

There have been attempts to improve the living conditions in the *favelas*. Parts of Rocinho, a *favela* in Rio, have been supplied with electricity and running water, but no

The densely populated *favelas* are breeding grounds for disease, crime and violence.

sewerage system. Most of the improvements have come from self-help projects, which cannot provide more than a few services. Rocinho organises walking tours for visitors, but most *favelas* are dangerous no-go areas, riddled with crime and ruled by drug traffickers and death squads. Many have long been abandoned by the authorities. In others, special police forces maintain some law and order.

CASE STUDY
STREET CHILDREN

Foraging for something to eat or sell is a daily chore for Brazil's street children.

As many as 12 million children in Brazil are forced to work instead of going to school. While most belong to *favela* families and return at night, others have no homes to go to. They sleep in doorways, under motorways and even in sewers. These are the *abandonados*, or 'deserted ones', Brazil's most tragic example of economic and social injustice.

Street children scrape a living doing whatever they can – selling goods, shining shoes, washing cars, stealing, or sifting through garbage. They are regularly exploited by adults, who use them as professional thieves, drug-runners or for prostitution. Brazil is estimated to have over half a million child prostitutes. There are reports of regular beatings by the authorities and, worst of all, murders carried out by paid vigilante groups. Charitable organisations such as UNICEF, the Red Cross and many religious groups do their best to help the situation but without parents, schools, food or jobs, most street children have no choice but crime.

NEW CITIES: BRASÍLIA AND BELO HORIZONTE

The Brazilian government has long been concerned with the problems caused by the country's unequal distribution and density of population. Vast areas of empty land are regarded as national security risks, and the over-concentration of people and wealth in regions like the Southeast is considered damaging to the country as a whole. In 1960, the national capital was moved from Rio de Janeiro to Brasília, 970km to the north-west, in an attempt to rebalance the population spread. The aim was to create a major growth pole in Brazil's sparsely populated heartland, but the new capital was also seen as an important status symbol, one of the most grandiose and expensive projects Brazil has undertaken.

LOCATING THE CAPITAL

The idea of a capital situated away from the coast was first suggested in 1789. A century later, in 1891, the concept was written into the new Republic's constitution, but it was not until 1952 that the scheme actually happened, following extensive air and other surveys to find a suitable site. The one chosen was a 581km^2 location in the state of Goias, a sparsely inhabited piece of *cerrado* land directly on the watershed between the Amazon and the Paraná river. Construction began in 1957 and the main government and administrative buildings were

completed in three years. Brasília was a new metropolis, a city without a history, and this was reflected in its futuristic plan and architecture, the work of Lucio Costa and Oscar Niemeyer. What distinguishes Brasília from cities that have grown naturally is the strict division between its functional zones: administration, business, housing, hotels and culture.

PLANS AND ARCHITECTURE

No one is certain whether the plan of Brasília was meant to resemble a cross, a bird or an aeroplane. Viewed from above it could be any of these (see city plan page 49). Since one of the first facilities to be completed was the airport (fast communications being essential), an aeroplane shape would have been a suitable choice. On its completion, the city's modern architecture caused a sensation, receiving both acclaim and criticism. UNESCO

Buildings like these apartment blocks have earned Brasília the description of 'an elegant monotonous city'.

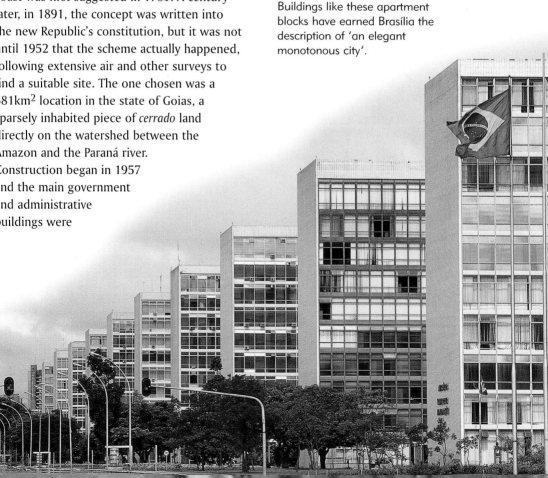

includes it as one of its world cultural heritage sites but others have been less enthusiastic, seeing it as 'elegant monotony' or the 'moon's backside'.

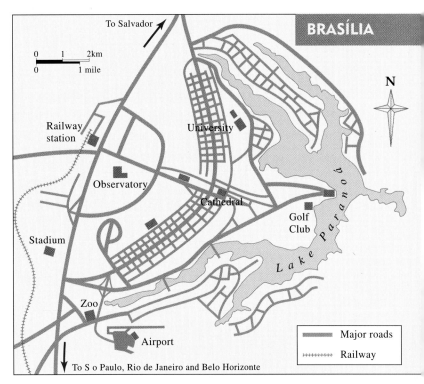

SUCCESS OR FAILURE?

Brasília's success is difficult to measure. Officially planned for a population of one million by 2000, this figure was reached by 1986, 14 years early. The new capital did help to shift the country's political and economic centre of gravity towards the north-west. However, there is much poverty in the city and the central area is ringed with large *favelas*, many of which started out as the temporary settlements of the construction workers. A comment by the planners puts Brasília into perspective: 'It was not designed to solve Brazil's problems. It was bound to reflect them'.

BELO HORIZONTE

Brasília was not the first modern Brazilian city to spring from a planner's drawing board. Belo Horizonte replaced the old colonial town of Ouro Preto in 1897 as the new state capital of Minas Gerais. Specially designed for its role, the city was laid out on a regular grid plan modelled on Washington DC. Today it is Brazil's third-largest city, a politically and culturally important centre. However its wide landscaped avenues and planned suburbs have suffered a high rate of urbanisation over the last 60 years and there are a large number of *favelas*. The city's name, meaning 'Beautiful Horizon', seems misplaced today considering the horizon is usually obscured by air pollution from its steel, car manufacturing and textile industries.

The 'Crown of Thorns' cathedral is one of Brasília's daringly different public buildings.

Recife's palm-fringed beaches and tropical climate help the Northeast's tourist industry.

Until recently, Brazil's tourist industry was poorly organised. Inadequate visitor facilities, high poverty levels and political troubles put off potential tourists. Another problem was the sheer distance of Brazil from the tourist supply region of the Northern Hemisphere, especially Western Europe. The neighbouring countries of Argentina and Uruguay have been Brazil's main source of tourists, with increasing numbers arriving from the USA. Most European tourists are Portuguese, Italian and German, reflecting the country's immigration history.

For many people, the thought of a holiday in Brazil conjures up images of cosmopolitan Rio de Janeiro and its famous carnival. Originally a purely religious festival held the week before Lent each year, this six-day party of music, dancing and costumed parades is celebrated throughout the country. But it is the Rio Carnival that is the most extravagant and world famous. Visitors from abroad and all over Brazil flock to the city every February, choking the airport, filling the hotels and inflating local prices. They are eager to be part of the world's largest and most colourful street festival.

Since the late 1970s EMBRATUR, the federal government tourism agency, has been encouraging tourism throughout the country. It recognises tourism as an important source of foreign currency and a way of improving Brazil's trade balance. As well as sponsoring city tourism, financial support is being given to beach resort development and to ecotourism in regions such as Amazonia.

RIO DE JANEIRO

Rio is Brazil's main entry point and tourism capital, with strong visitor attractions. The physical setting alone with its mountain peaks, Copacabana and Ipanema beaches, and tropical rain forest within the city limits more than justifies the title *Cidade Maravilhosa* ('Marvellous City'). Other attractions are the

Ecotourism in the Pantanal, where the activities of tourists are strictly controlled to prevent damage to the environment.

annual carnival held each year, sophisticated shopping districts, museums and monuments, and a lively nightlife.

BEACH RESORTS

The Northeast states see tourism as a way of developing their economies and of slowing down their population out-migration. Modern airports such as those at Fortaleza, Recife and Salvador have links with many international cities, and a recent trend has been the growth in charter flights and package holidays. Tourists are attracted by the region's extensive beaches. The state of Ceará alone has over 500km of coastline, much of it unspoilt, but other areas are rapidly developing as busy international resorts. This development can be seen in the area around Jericoacoara, once a down-market hippy centre whose beach is regarded as one of the world's most beautiful. It is still popular with backpackers but has recently attracted package holidaymakers staying in purpose-built hotels.

AMAZONIAN TOURISM

Uncontrolled tourism would be another threat to the Amazon rain forest. So far, visitor numbers have been limited and the many tourist agencies support ecotourism and forest sustainability. The famous Amazon Village is an eco-lodge on the shores of Lake Puraquequara, 30km from Manaus. Accommodation is in simple wooden bungalows and there is no electricity. Visitors can take trips into the rain forest and come into direct contact with its plants, animals and Amerindians.

HERITAGE TOURISM

Brazil has a rich heritage of colonial monuments ranging from forts, country houses and churches to entire old towns, which are now under protection. UNESCO has helped to promote their tourist appeal by making some of them world cultural heritage centres. The historic core of Salvador is an example.

From 1500 to 1815 Salvador was Brazil's busiest port, growing rich on sugar, gold and diamonds. Its wealth can be seen in the city's magnificent merchant houses and elaborate, gold-decorated churches. Olinda, a few kilometres north of Recife, is another protected town with sixteenth- and seventeenth-century churches and palaces. But it is Ouro Preto, the old state capital of Minas Gerais, that has Brazil's finest assembly of colonial architecture. The town has many Baroque churches set in an authentic townscape of unplanned, narrow and winding streets. The churches contain religious works of art by Brazil's famous architect and sculptor, Antonio Francisco Lisboa (1738–1814).

Tourism in the Amazon supports small-scale handicraft projects like this one, where money paid for the handicrafts goes straight to the people who made them.

The hi-tech equipment used in this São Paulo hospital is in sharp contrast to the average standard of medical equipment in Brazil.

QUALITY OF LIFE AND LEISURE

People's quality of life (their housing, diet, healthcare and income, for example) varies throughout Brazil. There are major differences in both rural and urban areas. The country's GNP per capita is low compared with developed countries, and there are vast inequalities in the distribution of wealth. The poorest 20 per cent of Brazil's population share only 2.5 per cent of the country's wealth. In comparison, the richest 20 per cent share between themselves 63.7 per cent of the total wealth.

A 'BELINDA' COUNTRY

Over 60 million Brazilians live in poverty. Many millions live without clean tap water, mains sewerage or proper health services.

Over 15 per cent of the country's youngest children suffer from malnutrition. In some areas, infant mortality is 40 times higher than the average for Europe. A third of the population is illiterate. For these and other reasons, Brazil has been described as 'Belinda', a country with an economic potential similar to Belgium but with social problems similar to parts of India. In Brazil, a small affluent First-World society lives alongside those trapped in a Third-World cycle of poverty.

EDUCATION AND HEALTH

The low priority given to education is a key factor explaining Brazil's poverty. Many rural and urban children have never attended school, or leave at the earliest opportunity without qualifications. It is estimated that some 40 per cent of Brazilians over 15 are not capable of reading and understanding a newspaper. This means that there are few possibilities of them finding work except in menial and poorly paid jobs. The uneducated are trapped in a disadvantaged lifestyle.

Poor health services do not help. Those who can afford it have access to advanced medical facilities, but for the rest of the population there is a chronic shortage of medical

Brazil needs to spend more money on schools to improve its literacy levels.

A carnival procession by a Candomblé religious group in Salvador. The Candomblé religion combines elements of West African and Christian faiths.

personnel, hospitals and medicines. Travelling bus and riverboat clinics provide medical help in remote areas, but the poor get little treatment for diseases such as cholera, pesticide poisoning or, increasingly, AIDS.

LEISURE TIME
As in all countries there is a firm link in Brazil between leisure activities and available wealth. Some of the biggest differences are seen in the major cities, where the wealthy enjoy an affluent life of restaurants, bars and night clubs that are beyond the reach of a large section of the population. There are, however, certain activities in which all Brazilians can take part, irrespective of social class and financial status.

Football is Brazil's most popular leisure activity. The game is played everywhere – on beaches, in the streets and on any piece of vacant ground. It is watched by millions on television or in huge stadiums such as Rio's Maracaná, which has a crowd capacity of 150,000. Many young Brazilians dream of becoming football stars. In coastal cities such as Rio and Salvador, Brazil also has a well-developed beach culture. Beach activities include volleyball, which is another popular Brazilian sport.

RELIGION
Many Brazilian festivals and holidays are related to religion. Although Brazil claims to have the largest Catholic population of any country in the world, there are a great variety of other religions. Some religions, such as Candomblé, Umbanda and Macumba, combine elements from a number of different faiths. The main influences are from Amerindian beliefs, Christianity and African religions brought to Brazil during the slave era. Many Brazilians practise their own individualised religion, including Christian saints, Indian idols and African deities in their worship and prayers.

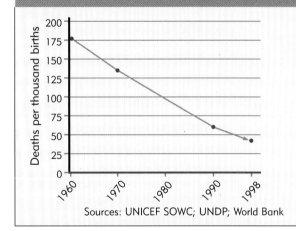

UNDER-FIVE MORTALITY RATE

Deaths per thousand births

Sources: UNICEF SOWC; UNDP; World Bank

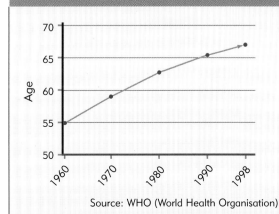

LIFE EXPECTANCY AT BIRTH

Age

Source: WHO (World Health Organisation)

BRAZIL AND THE WORLD

The dam at the Itaipú hydroelectric power station cost over US$25 billion.

Despite its huge size and population, Brazil has not played a major political role in shaping the world. Economically, however, especially with products such as rubber, sugar, coffee and minerals, it has long been linked to the world economy. Today the processes of globalisation affect almost every aspect of the country's economic and social life. Much is related to the fact that Brazil owes vast sums of money to foreign banks and financial institutions.

NATIONAL DEBT

Between 1964 and 1985, when the military governed the country, Brazil borrowed huge amounts of money from abroad. The money was used to build roads, hydroelectric power stations, the new capital of Brasília, and to search for minerals. The borrowing helped the country's economic progress, but much was wasted on poorly planned, large-scale projects instead of being spent on education, housing and medical services. In 1999, the Brazilian national debt was quoted as US$232 billion. This is the equivalent of US$1,399 for every Brazilian man, woman and child.

Many argue that Brazil's national debt has increased the country's social and economic

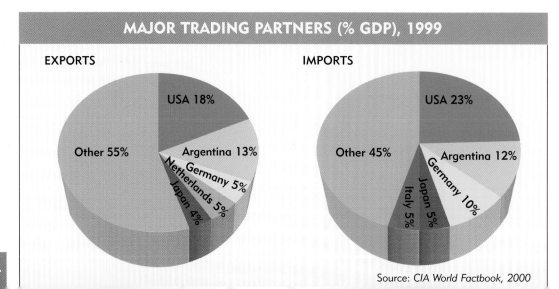

MAJOR TRADING PARTNERS (% GDP), 1999

EXPORTS

USA 18%
Argentina 13%
Germany 5%
Netherlands 5%
Japan 4%
Other 55%

IMPORTS

USA 23%
Argentina 12%
Germany 10%
Japan 5%
Italy 5%
Other 45%

Source: CIA World Factbook, 2000

inequalities. Repayment to foreign banks has to be paid by about 70 per cent of Brazilian exports, and constantly rising interest rates have increased this burden. As an alternative method of repayment, banks have agreed to receive company and other investment shares in Brazilian businesses. This leads to further global involvement in the country's economy.

TRADING PARTNERS

Brazil's main trading links are, in descending order, with the EU, North America, Asia and the Middle East. As the wealthiest country in South America, it has a big influence on improving the whole continent's economy. An important part of South American trade is through MERCOSUL, a union currently linking Brazil, Argentina, Paraguay and Uruguay, where each country can trade with each other free of tax. This makes the imported products cheaper than imports from Western countries, so it helps countries in the union. Other South American countries are interested in joining this 'common market', whose goal is to create a trade area which is less dependant on Western countries.

SPORTING WORLD

Brazil is often in the world's headlines for its sporting achievements. Mention Brazil and many people will think of football. Even those little interested in the game will have heard of

Products from small-scale organic farms, like this organic pepper farm in Bahia, fetch higher prices in Brazil than products sold to the international market.

Brazilian players, not least Pelé (Edson Arantes do Nascimento), internationally acclaimed as one of the world's greatest soccer players. The Brazilian team has been the first to win the World Cup four times, in 1958, 1962, 1970 and 1994. To win is a great source of national pride; to lose is a national disaster.

Another of Brazil's major contributions to the sporting world is its success in motor racing, with names such as Emerson Fittipaldi, Nelson Piquet and Ayrton Senna. Since the 1970s, Brazil has won more Formula One Grand Prix championships than any other country.

MUSIC

It is said that the Brazilians are among the most musical people in the world. The country's popular music, shaped by the rhythms of three continents, has achieved international success. The samba (hallmark of the Rio carnival), bossa nova, lambada and other musical styles have taken the sounds and atmosphere of Brazil to all parts of the world.

Hundreds gather to watch the football World Cup on a huge outdoor screen.

LAND OF THE FUTURE

Some people say that 'Brazil is the land of the future.' From the arrival of the first Europeans in the early sixteenth century, Brazil's vast South American territory has been a land of great opportunity. Land, forests, water and minerals provided great potential for many rich lifestyles. Yet compared with modern industrialised countries, Brazil is still a poor nation, and there is a huge gap between the rich and the poor.

In the countryside and the cities, Brazil's wealthy live in large, closely guarded mansions and villas. They move around in chauffeur-driven cars and often have armed bodyguards to protect them from kidnappers. In contrast are the country's urban slums overcrowded with undernourished youngsters. This gap between rich and poor is because Brazil has always been dominated, both economically and politically, by a small, influential elite. Despite important changes of government, this minority still controls the country. The elite own huge areas of land, and since land equals wealth in Brazil, this is a major cause of social inequality. Until there are major land reforms and redistribution, Brazil's social inequality will continue.

Only a small proportion of Brazilians can shop in stores like these. The struggle to close the gap between rich and poor is one of Brazil's biggest challenges.

CONSERVATION AND THE ENVIRONMENT

In its natural state, the Amazon rain forest is an almost perfectly closed ecosystem, but it can easily be disrupted by outside pressures. Many authorities consider the results of rain-forest interference to be the world's most serious land-use problem. But Amazonia is not the only region of threatened habitats. Brazil's Atlantic forest, home of the tamarin monkeys and other endangered species, has been reduced to some 7 per cent of its original cover. The rest has been taken over by cattle pastures, cultivation and urbanisation. As in other parts of Brazil, scientists are calling for an increase in eco-agriculture, a way of increasing food production through new land use policies rather than encroaching into natural areas.

In June 1992, an international conference about the environment was held in Rio, called the Rio Summit. Reports from the conference stressed the importance of Brazil

PERSONAL COMPUTERS

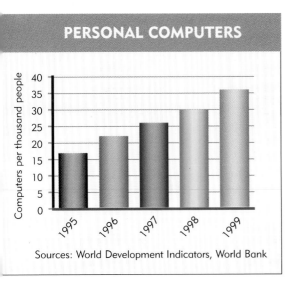

Computers per thousand people (y-axis, 0 to 40)

Years: 1995, 1996, 1997, 1998, 1999

Sources: World Development Indicators, World Bank

RIGHT: Without basic education or skills, people earn money in any way they can.

to the protection of the world environment. The conference made it clear that many countries are responsible for what is happening in Amazonia, where interference with the region's ecosystems have led to the 'greenhouse effect' and 'global warming'. The same issues were raised at the 2001 Kyoto Protocol in Japan. It was made clear that protection of Brazil's environment must be the responsibility of the world, as well as Brazil, if the world climate is to be protected in the future.

The uakari monkey is just one of many species threatened by development in the Amazon.

BRAZIL'S PEOPLE – A VALUABLE RESOURCE

With about 70 per cent of its population under the age of 30, Brazil's young nation is full of new ideas, dreams and boundless energy. Together with its natural resources, a rapidly developing financial sector and a core of educated business managers, Brazil has the potential to become a major world power.

Agrarian To do with land and its farming use.

Agribusinesses Businesses associated with farming, for example, farmhouse tourism.

Baroque A style of art and architecture that flourished between the sixteenth and eighteenth centuries.

Black market The exchange of illegally acquired and traded goods.

Cash crop A crop grown for sale rather than local use.

Colony A community formed by settlers in a country that is far from their homeland.

Coniferous Trees that bear cones and are usually evergreen.

Constitution The agreed basic principles of a formal organisation such as a national government.

Consumer goods Manufactured goods to be sold directly to people, such as clothes and food.

Conurbations Large urban areas created by the linking together of several towns.

Dictatorship A form of government in which an individual, committee, or a group holds absolute power.

Drainage basin The area that is drained by a river and its tributaries.

Ecologists People who are specialists in ecology, the study of the relationship of plants and animals to their environment.

Ecosystem A community of plants and animals, and the environment in which they live.

Ecotourism A type of tourism that tries to protect the environment.

Elite A small number of rich and powerful people or organisations.

Favelas Shanty towns, or slums.

Favelados The Brazilian name for people who live in the *favelas*, or shanty towns.

Federal government A system of government in which political power is divided between a central government and smaller units, such as states.

GDP Gross Domestic Product is the volume of goods and services produced annually in a country, but excluding earnings from overseas.

Global warming The gradual warming of the surface of the planet as a result of a change in the composition of atmospheric gases, especially an increase in the percentage of carbon dioxide.

GMT Greenwich Mean Time, the time at Greenwich, England, which was made the starting point of the world's time zones in 1884.

GNP Gross National Product is the volume of goods and services produced annually within a country, which includes earnings from overseas.

Greenhouse gases Gases that help to trap warmth in the atmosphere, which contributes to global warming.

Growth pole A region where the growth of industries and development has caused other growth in a chain reaction.

Hi-tech industries High technology industries. These are industries that use the latest production techniques and technology, such as aerospace, computing and electronics.

Hydroelectric power stations Structures designed to generate electricity by using the power of water.

Inflation A general increase in prices.

Intensive farming A type of farming that requires a high level of labour and money.

Microclimate The local climate of a very small part of the world.

Migrant A person who moves away from his or her home. The move can be temporary, like a period of working abroad, or permanent.

Monoculture Concentrating on a single product on a farm.

Multinationals Large companies that have factories or offices in more than one country.

Pampas The name given to the mostly treeless plains of South America south of the Amazon.

Population structure The numbers and proportion of people in particular age-groups within a population.

Primary forest The original forest cover of an area.

Privatisation Ownership by individuals rather than the government.

Quality of life The level of economic, social and environmental satisfaction experienced by a person or community.

Rhea A large flightless bird, similar to the ostrich.

Savanna Another name for pampas.

Scrubland An area of dry poor soil supporting stunted trees and shrubs, as in the Brazilian *sertão*.

Secondary forest Forest that grows once the original trees have been cut down.

Sertão Back country (see also Scrubland).

Trade balance A country's profit or loss from the value of its imports and exports.

Tropical climate A climate of constant high temperatures and rainfall found between the Tropics of Capricorn and Cancer.

UNESCO United Nations Educational, Scientific and Cultural Organisation, a part of the United Nations which promotes education, communication and the arts.

Urbanisation The growth of urban areas.

Watershed The area separating streams that flow into different drainage basins.

FURTHER INFORMATION

BOOKS TO READ:

Antonio's Rain Forest by Anna Lewington & Edward Parker (Hodder Wayland, 1998) Looks at the life of a rubber tapper's son in the Amazon.

At Home in the Street: Street Children of Northeast Brazil by Tobias Hecht (Cambridge University Press, 1998) Based on fieldwork among the children themselves, this book examines the lives of Brazilian street children.

Atlas of Rain Forests by Anna Lewington (Hodder Wayland, 1999) Looks at peoples, plants and animals in rain forests around the world.

The Changing Face of Brazil by Edward Parker (Hodder Wayland, 2001) Illustrated reference for KS2.

Country Fact Files: Brazil by Marion Morrison (Hodder Wayland, 1997) Illustrated reference for KS3.

Country Studies: Brazil by Roger Robinson (Heinemann Educational Secondary Division, 1997) Illustrated reference for GCSE, including statistics and case studies.

Exploring Brazil by Chris Smart & Steve Lockwood (Hodder & Stoughton Educational, 1994) In-depth study of Brazil for KS3 and foundation GCSE level.

The Rough Guide to Brazil (Rough Guides, 2000) A comprehensive handbook to Brazil, with practical tips and region-by-region commentary.

Secrets of the Rainforest series by Michael Chinery (Cherrytree, 1999–2000) Titles on people, plants, animals and conservation issues in tropical rain forests.

The Street Children of Brazil by Sarah de Carvalho (Hodder & Stoughton Religious, 1996) Follows an Englishwoman's experience of working for a missionary organisation in Brazil helping street children.

Wealth of Nations: Brazil by Jen Green (Hodder Wayland, 2001) Illustrated reference for KS2–3.

WEBSITES:

GENERAL INFORMATION ON BRAZIL
Brazilinfo.com
http://www.brazilinfo.com
Click on the British flag for the English version of this site, which provides general information on Brazil including features on its national parks, history and general statistics.

Brazilian Embassy
http://www.brazil.org.uk/

GENERAL STATISTICS
Brazil: the World Factbook:
http://www.cia.gov/cia/publications/factbook/geos/br

SÃO PAULO
São Paulo State Government
http://www.saopaulo.sp.gov.br/home/index.htm
Click on the English version icon for information on tourism, culture and the history of São Paulo.

RIO DE JANEIRO
Rio State Government
http://www.governo.rj.gov.br
Click on the English version icon.

Jaguars live in the rain forests of Brazil, but they are becoming increasingly rare.

Rio de Janeiro's most famous landmark – the statue of Christ the Redeemer – shrouded in mist.